ELEMENTS OF DEBATING

o

Elements of Debating

A Manual for Use in High Schools and Academies

By

LEVERETT S. LYON

*Head of the Department of Civic Science in the
Joliet Township High School*

THE UNIVERSITY OF CHICAGO PRESS
CHICAGO, ILLINOIS
1913

TO
THE MEMORY OF
M. M. L.

PREFACE

This book pretends but little to originality in material. Its aim is to offer the old in a form that shall meet the needs of young students who are beginning work in debate. The effort has been made only to present the elements of forensic work so freed from technicality that they may be apparent to the student with the greatest possible economy of time and the least possible interpretation by the teacher.

It is hoped that the book may serve not only those schools where debating is a part of the regular course, but also those institutions where it is a supplement to the work in English or is encouraged as a "super-curriculum" activity.

Although the general obligation to other writers is obvious, there is no specific indebtedness not elsewhere acknowledged, except to Mr. Arthur Edward Phillips, whose vital principle of "Reference to Experience" has, in a modified form, been made the test for evidence. It is my belief that the use of this principle, rather than the logical and technical forms of proof and evidence, will make the training of debate far more applicable in other forms of public speaking. My special thanks are due to Miss Charlotte Van Der Veen and Miss Elizabeth Barns, whose aid has added technical exactness to almost every page. I wish

to thank also Miss Bella Hopper for suggestions in
preparing the reference list of Appendix I. Most
of all, I am indebted to the students whose interest
has been a constant stimulus, and whose needs have
been to me, as they are to all who teach, the one
sure and constant guide.

L. S. L.

TABLE OF CONTENTS

LESSON I

WHAT ARGUMENTATION IS

I. The purpose of discourse
II. The forms of discourse:
    1. Narration
    2. Description
    3. Exposition
    4. Argumentation

When we pause to look about us and to realize what things are really going on, we discern that everyone is talking and writing. Perhaps we wonder why this is the case. Nature is said to be economical. She would hardly have us make so much effort and use so much energy without some purpose, and some purpose beneficial to us. So we determine that the purpose of using language is to convey meaning, to give ideas that we have to someone else.

As we watch a little more closely, we see that in talking or writing we are not merely talking or writing something. We see that everyone, consciously or unconsciously, clearly or dimly, is always trying to do some definite thing. Let us see what the things are which we may be trying to do.

If you should tell your father, when you return from school, how Columbus discovered America on October 12, 1492, and should try to make him see the scene on shipboard when land was first sighted as clearly as you see it, you would be describing. That kind of discourse would be called description. Its purpose is to make another see in his mind's eye the same image or picture that we have in our own.

On the other hand, if you wished to tell him the story of the discovery of America, you would do something quite different. You would tell him not only of the first sight of land, but of the whole series of incidents which led up to that event. If he could follow you readily, could almost live through the various happenings that you related, you would be telling your story well. That kind of discourse is not description but narration.

Suppose, then, that your father should say: "Now tell me this: What is the difference between the discovery of America and the colonization of America?" You would now have a new task. You would not care to make him see any particular scene or live through the events of discovery but to make him *understand something which you understand.* You would show him that the discovery of America meant merely the fact that America was found to be here, but that colonization meant the coming, not of the explorers, but of the permanent settlers. This form of discourse which makes clear to someone else an idea that is already clear to us is called exposition.

And now suppose your father should say: "Well, you have told me a great deal which I may say is interesting enough, but it seems to me rather useless. What is the purpose of all this study? Why have you spent so much time learning of this one event?" You would of course answer: "Because the discovery of America was an event of great importance."

He might reply: "I still do not believe that." Then you would say: "I'll prove it to you," or, "I'll convince you of it." You would then have undertaken to do what you are now trying to learn how to do better—to argue. *For argumentation is that form of discourse that we use when we attempt to make some one else believe as we wish him to believe.* "Argumentation is the art of producing in the mind of someone else a belief in the ideas which the speaker or writer wishes the hearer or reader to accept."[1]

You made use of argumentation when you urged a friend to take the course in chemistry in your school by trying to make him believe it would be beneficial to him. You used argumentation when you urged a friend to join the football squad by trying to make him believe, as you believe, that the exercise would do him good. A minister uses argumentation when he tries to make his congregation believe, as he believes, that ten minutes spent in prayer each morning will make the day's work easier. The salesman uses argumentation to sell his goods. The chance of the merchant to recover a rebate on a bill of goods that he believes are

[1] Baker, *Principles of Argumentation.*

defective depends entirely on his ability to make the seller believe the same thing. On argumentation the lawyer bases his hope of making the jury believe that his client is innocent of crime. All of us every day of our lives, in ordinary conversation, in our letters, and in more formal talks, are trying to make others believe as we wish them to believe. Our success in so doing depends upon our skill in the art of argumentation.

SUGGESTED EXERCISES

1. Out of your study or reading of the past week, give an illustration of: (1) narration; (2) description; (3) exposition; (4) argumentation.

2. During the past week, on what occasions have you personally made use of: (1) narration; (2) description; (3) exposition; (4) argumentation?

3. Explain carefully the distinction between description and exposition. In explaining this distinction, what form of discourse have you used?

4. Define argumentation.

5. Skill in argumentation is a valuable acquisition for:

(Give three reasons)

(1)...

(2)...

(3)...

LESSON II

WHAT DEBATE IS

I. The forms of argumentation:
   1. Written.
   2. Oral.

II. The forms of oral argumentation:
   1. General discussion.
   2. Debate.

III. The qualities of debate:
   1. Oral.
   2. Judges present.
   3. Prescribed conditions.
   4. Decision expected.

Now, since we have decided upon a definition of argumentation, let us see what we mean by the term "debate" as it will be used in this work.

We have said that argumentation is the art of producing in the mind of someone a belief in something in which we wish him to believe.

Now it is obvious that this can be accomplished in different ways. Perhaps the most common method of attempting to bring someone to believe as we wish is the oral method. On your way to school you meet a friend and assert your belief that in the coming football game the home team will win. You continue: "Our team has already beaten teams that have defeated our opponent of

5

next Saturday, and, moreover, our team is stronger than it has been at any time this season." When you finish, your friend replies: "I believe you are right. We shall win."

You have been carrying on oral argumentation.

If, when you had finished, your friend had not agreed with you, your effort would have been none the less argumentation, only it would have been unsuccessful. If you had written the same thing to your friend in a letter, your letter would have been argumentative.

Suppose your father were running for an office and should make a public speech. If he tried to make the audience believe that the best way to secure lower taxes, better water, and improved streets would be through his election, he would be making use of oral argumentation. If he should do the same thing through newspaper editorials, he would be using written argumentation.

Argumentation, then, may be carried on either in writing or orally, and may vary from the informality of an ordinary conversation or a letter to a careful address or thoughtful article.

What, then, is debate as we shall use the word in this work, and what is the relation of argumentation to debate? The term "debate" in its general use has, of course, many senses. You might say: "I had a debate with a friend about the coming football game." Or your father might say: "I heard the great Lincoln and Douglas debates before the Civil War." Although both of you would be using the term as it is generally used, you would not be using it as it will be used in this book, or as it is best that a student of argumentation and debate should use it.

The term "debate," in the sense in which students of these subjects should use it, means *oral argumentation carried on by two opposing teams under certain prescribed regulations, and with the expectation of having a decision rendered by judges who are present.* This is "debate" used, not generally, as you used it in saying, "I debated with a friend," but technically, as we use it when we refer to the Yale-Harvard debate or the Northern Debating League. In order to keep the meaning of this term clearly in mind, use it only when referring to such contests as these. In speaking of your argumentative conversation with your friend or of the forensic contests between Lincoln and Douglas, use the term "discussion" rather than "debate."

It is true that the controversy between Lincoln and Douglas conformed to our definition of "debate" in being oral; moreover, at least in sense, two teams (of one man each) competed, but there were no judges, and no direct decision was rendered.

Since argumentation, then, is the art of producing in the mind of someone else a belief in the idea or ideas you wish to convey, and debate is an argumentative contest carried on orally under certain conditions, it is clear that argumentation is the broader term of the two and that debate is merely a specialized kind of argumentation. Football is exercise, but there is exercise in many other forms. Debate is argumentation, but one can also find argumentation in many other forms.

The following diagram makes clear the work we have covered thus far. It shows the relation between argumentation and debate, and shows that the specialized term "debate" has the same relation to "discourse" that "football" has to "exercise."

Kinds of exercise {
  Play {
    Miscellaneous
    Swimming
    Skating
    Rolling hoop
    Athletic games { Other athletic games / Football
  Work
}

Kinds of discourse {
  Description
  Narration
  Exposition
  Argumentation { Written / Oral { General discussion / Debate
}

Suggested Exercises

1. Be prepared to explain orally in class, as though to *someone who did not know*, the difference between "argumentation" and "debate."

2. Set down three conditions that must exist before argumentation becomes debate.

3. Have you ever argued? Orally? In writing?

4. Have you ever debated? Did you win?

5. Which is the broader term, "argumentation," or "debate?" Why?

6. Compose some sentences, illustrating the use of the terms "debate" and "argumentation."

LESSON III

THE REQUIREMENTS OF SUCCESSFUL DEBATING

I. The three requirements stated.

II. How to make clear to the audience what one wishes them to believe, by:

    1. Stating the idea which one wishes to have accepted in the form of a definite assertion, which is:

        (1) Interesting.

        (2) Definite and concise.

        (3) Single in form.

        (4) Fair to both sides.

    2. Defining the "terms of the question" so that they will be:

        (1) Clear.

        (2) Convincing.

        (3) Consistent with the origin and history of the question.

    3. Restating the whole question in the light of the definitions.

To debate successfully it is necessary to do three things:

1. To make perfectly clear to your audience what you wish them to believe.

2. To show them why the proof of certain points (called issues) should make them believe the thing you wish them to believe.

3. To prove the issues.

Each of these three things is a distinct process, involving several steps. One is as important as another.

9

It is impossible to prove the issues until we have found them, but equally impossible to show the audience what the issues are until we have shown what the thing is which we wish those issues to support. First, then, let us see what we mean by making perfectly clear what you wish to have the audience believe.

Suppose that you should meet a friend who says to you: "I am going to argue with you about examinations." You might naturally reply: "What examinations?" If he should say, "All examinations: the honor system in all examinations," you might very reasonably still be puzzled and ask if by all examinations he meant examinations of every kind in grade school, high school, and college, as well as the civil service examinations, and what was meant by the honor system.

He would now probably explain to you carefully how several schools have been experimenting with the idea of giving all examinations without the presence of a teacher or monitor of any sort. During these examinations, however, it has been customary to ask the students themselves to report any cheating that they may observe. It is also required that each student state in writing, at the end of his paper, upon honor, that he has neither given nor received aid during the test. "To this method," your friend continues, "has been given the name of the honor system. And I believe that this system should be adopted in all examinations in the Greenburg High School."

He has now stated definitely what he wishes to make you believe, and he has done more; he has explained to you the meaning of the terms that you did not understand. These two things make perfectly clear to you what he wishes you to believe, and he has thus covered the first step in argumentation.

From this illustration, then, several rules can be drawn. In the first place your friend stated that he wished to argue about examinations. Why could he not begin his argument at once? Because he had not yet asked you to believe anything about examinations. He might have said, "I am going to explain examinations," and he could then have told you what examinations were. That would have been exposition. But he could not *argue* until he had made a definite assertion about the term "examination."

Rule one would then be: State in the form of a definite assertion the matter to be argued.

In order to be suitable for debating, an assertion or, as it is often called, proposition, of this kind should conform to certain conditions:

1. It should be one in which both the debaters and the audience are interested. Failure to observe this rule has caused many to think debating a dry subject.

2. It should propose something different from existing conditions. Argument should have an end in view. Your school has no lunchroom. Should it have one? Your city is governed by a mayor and a council. Should it be ruled by a

commission? Merely to debate, as did the men of the Middle Ages, how many angels could dance on the point of a needle, or, as some more modern debaters have done, whether Grant was a greater general than Washington, is useless.

The fact that those on the affirmative side propose something new places on them what is called the *burden of proof*. This means that they must show why there is *need* of a change from the present state of things. When they have done this, they may proceed to argue in favor of the *particular change* which they propose.

3. It should make a single statement about a single thing:

(Correct)　In public high schools secret societies should be prohibited.

(Incorrect)　In public high schools and colleges secret societies and teaching of the Bible should be prohibited.

4. It must be expressed with such definiteness that both sides can agree on what it means.

5. It must be expressed in such a way as to be fair to both sides.

But you noticed that your friend had not only to state the question definitely, but to explain what the terms of the proposition meant. He had to tell you what the "honor system" was.

Our second rule, then, for making the question clear, is: In the proposition as stated, explain all terms that may not be entirely clear to your audience.

And in explaining or defining these terms, there are certain things that you must do. You must make the definition clear, or it will be no better than the term itself. This is not always easy. In defining "moral force" a gentleman said: "Why, moral force is er-er-moral force." He did not get very far on the way toward making his term clear. Be sure that your definition really explains the term.

Then one must be careful not to define in a circle. Let us take, for example, the assertion or proposition, "The development of labor unions has been beneficial to commerce." If you should attempt to define "development" by saying "development means growth," you would not have made the meaning of the term much clearer; and if in a further attempt to explain it, you could only add "And growth means development," you would be defining in a circle.

There is still another error to be avoided in making your terms clear to your audience. This error is called begging the question. This occurs when a term is defined in such a way that there is nothing left to be argued.

Suppose your friend should say to you: "I wish to make you believe that the honor system should be used in all examinations in the Greenburg High School." You ask him what he means by the "honor system." He replies: "I mean the best system in the world." Is there anything left to argue? Hardly, if his definition of the term honor system is correct, for it would be very irrational indeed to disagree with the assertion that the best system in the world should be adopted in the Greenburg High School.

To summarize: *Define terms carefully;* make the definition clear; do not define in a circle, and do not beg the question.

As you have already noticed, terms in argumentation, such as "honor system," often consist of more than one word. They sometimes contain several words. "A term [as that word is used in debating and argumentation] may consist of any number of names, substantive or objective, with the articles, prepositions, and conjunctions required to join them together; still it is only one term if it points out or makes us think of only one thing or object or class of objects."[1] In such cases a dictionary is of little use. Take the term "honor system," the meaning of which was not clear to you. A dictionary offers no help. How is the student who wishes to discuss this question to decide upon the meaning of the term? Notice how your friend made it clear to you. He gave a history of the question that he wished to argue. He showed how the term "honor system" came into use and what it means where that system of examinations is in vogue. This, then, is the only method of making sure of the meaning of a term: to study the history of the question and see what the term means in the light of that history. This

[1] Jevons, *Primer of Logic.*

method has the added advantage that a term defined in this way will not only be entirely clear to your audience, but will also tend to convince them.

A dispute may arise between yourself and an opponent as to the meaning of a term. He may be relying on a dictionary or the statement of a single writer, while you are familiar with the history of the question. Under those circumstances it will be easy for you to show the judges and the audience that, although he may be using the term correctly in a general way, he is quite wrong when the special question under discussion is considered.

To make this more clear, let us take a specific instance. Suppose that you are debating the proposition, "Football Should Be Abolished in This High School." Football, as defined in the dictionary, differs considerably from the game with which every American boy is familiar. Further, the dictionary defines both the English and the American game. If your opponent should take either of these definitions, he would not have much chance of convincing an American audience that it was correct. Or if he should define football according to the rules of the game as it was played five or ten years ago, he would be equally ineffective.

You, on the other hand, announce that in your discussion you will use the term "football" as that game is described in *Spaulding's present year's rule book for the American game*, and that every reference you make to plays allowed or forbidden will be on the basis of the latest ruling. You then have a definition based on the history of the question. As you can see, the case for or against English football would be different from that of the American game. In the same way the case for or against football as it was played ten years ago would be very different from the case of football as it is played today.

All this does not mean that definitions found in dictionaries or other works of reference are never good; it means simply that such definitions should not be taken as final until the question has been carefully reviewed. Try to think out for yourself the meaning of the question. Decide what it involves and how it has arisen, or could arise in real life. Then, when you do outside reading on the subject, keep this same idea in mind. Keep asking yourself: "How did this question arise? Why is it being discussed?" You will be surprised to find that when you are ready to answer that question you will have most of your reading done, for you will have read most of the arguments upon it. Then you are ready to make it clear to the audience.

When you have thus given a clear and convincing definition of all the terms, it is a good plan to restate the whole question in the light of those definitions.

For instance, notice the question of the "honor system." The original question might have been concisely stated: "All Examinations in the Greenburg High School Should Be Conducted under the Honor System."

After you have made clear what you mean by the "honor system," you will be ready to restate the question as follows: "The question then is this: No Teacher Shall Be Present during Any Examination in the Greenburg High School, and Every Student Shall Be Required to State on Honor That He Has Neither Given Nor Received Aid in the Examinations."

Your hearers will now see clearly what you wish them to believe.

Thus far, then, we have seen that to debate well we should have a question which is of interest to ourselves and to the audience. The first step toward success is to make clear to our hearers the proposition presented for their acceptance. This may be done

1) By stating the idea that we wish them to accept in the form of an assertion, which should be:

   a) interesting
   b) definite and concise
   c) single in form
   d) fair to both sides

2) By defining the "terms of the question" so that they will be:

   a) clear
   b) convincing
   c) consistent with the origin and history of the question

3) By restating the whole question in the light of our definitions.

Suggested Exercises

1. State the three processes of successful debating.

2. What are the three necessary steps in the first process?

3. What qualities should a proposition for debate possess?

4. Give a proposition that you think has these qualities.

5. Without reference to books, define all the terms of this proposition. Follow the rules but make the definitions as brief as possible.

6. Make some propositions in which the following terms shall be used: (1) "Athletics," (2) "This City," (3) "All Studies," (4) "Manual Training," (5) "Domestic Science."

7. Point out the weakness in the following propositions (consider propositions always with your class as the audience):

(1) "Physics, Chemistry, and Algebra Are Hard Studies."

(2) "Only Useful Studies Should Be Taught in This School."

(3) "All Women Should Be Allowed to Vote and Should Be Compelled by Law to Remove Their Hats in Church."

(4) "Agricultural Conditions in Abyssinia Are Superior to Those in Burma."

8. Compare the dictionary definition of the following terms with the meaning which the history of the question has given them in actual usage:

(1) Domestic science.

(2) Aeroplane exhibitions.

(3) The international Olympic games.

(4) Township high schools.

(5) National conventions of political parties.

LESSON IV

DETERMINING THE ISSUES

I. What the "issues" are.
II. How to determine the issues.
III. The value of correct issues.

When you have made perfectly clear to your hearers what you wish them to believe, the next step is to show them why they should believe it. The first step in this process, as we saw at the beginning of Lesson III, is to see what points, if proved, will make them believe it.

These points, as we call them, are better known as "issues." The issues are really questions, the basic questions on which your side and the other disagree. The negative would answer "No" to these issues, the affirmative would say "Yes."

The issues when stated in declarative sentences are the fundamental reasons why the affirmative believes its proposition should be believed.

A student might be arguing with himself whether he would study law or medicine. He would say to himself: "These are the issues: For which am I the better adapted? Which requires the more study? Which offers the better promise of reward? In which can I do the more good?"

Should he argue with a friend in order to induce him to give up law and to study medicine, he would use similar issues. He would feel that if he could settle these questions he could convince his friend. Now, however, he would state them as declarative sentences and say: "You are more adapted to the profession of medicine; you can do more good in this field," etc. If the friend should open the question, he would be in the position of a man on the negative side of a debate. He would state the issues negatively as his reasons. He would say: "I am not so well adapted to the study of medicine; it offers less promise of reward," etc.

Each of these would in turn depend upon other reasons, but every proposition will depend for its acceptance on the proof of a few main issues. Perhaps this point can be made clearer by an illustration. Suppose we should take hold of one small rod which we see in the framework of a large truss bridge and should say: "This bridge is strong because this rod is here." Our statement would be only partially true. The rod might be broken, and although the strength of the bridge as a whole might be slightly weakened, it would not fall. But suppose we should say: "This bridge really rests on these four great steel beams which run down to the stone abutment. If I can see that these four steel beams are secure, I can believe in the security of the bridge." So a mechanical engineer shows us that certain rods and bars of the framework hold up one beam, and how similar rods and bars sustain a second, and that yet other rods and bars distribute the weight that would press too heavily on a third, and so at last we are convinced that the bridge is safe. It is not because we have been shown that several of the bolts and braces are strong, but because we have been shown that the four great beams, upon which it rests, are reliable.

Thus it is with everything in which we believe. We do not believe that taxes are just because the government must have money to pay the president or to buy uniforms for the army officers. These things must be done, but they are incidentals. They are facts, but they are like the small braces of the bridge. We believe that taxation is just, because the government must have money for its work. Paying the president and buying uniforms are details of this more fundamental reason.

In the same way we might say: "Athletics should be encouraged in high schools because it will make John Brown, who will participate, more healthy." That is a reason, but again only a small supporting reason. We might rather choose a fundamental reason, which this slight reason would in turn support, and it would be: "Athletics should be encouraged in high schools because they improve the health of the students that participate."

In a recent debate between two large high schools on the proposition: "*Resolved*, That Contests within High Schools Should Be Substituted for Contests between High Schools," one of the contesting teams took the following as issues:

1. Contests within high schools will accomplish the real purpose of contests better than will contests between schools.

2. Contests within high schools are the more democratic.

3. Contests within high schools can be made to work successfully.

When these three facts had been demonstrated, there was little left to urge against the claim.

Recently among the universities of a certain section, this question was discussed: *"Resolved, That the Federal Government Should Levy a Graduated Income Tax."* (Such tax was conceded as constitutional.) One university decided upon these as the issues:

1. Does the government need additional revenue?

2. Admitting that additional revenue is needed, is a graduated income tax the best way of securing the money?

3. Could a graduated income tax be successfully collected?

Here again if the debaters favoring a graduated income could show that the government does need the money, that the proposed tax is the best way to get it, and that such a tax would work in practice, they would make the audience believe their proposition. If the speakers on the negative side could show that the income of the federal government is sufficient, that, even if additional revenue is needed, this is a poor way to obtain it, or that this plan, though good in theory, is impracticable, they would have a good case. Thus in every question that is two-sided enough to be a good question for debate, there are certain fundamental issues upon which the disagreement between the affirmative and the negative can be shown to rest. When either side has answered "Yes" or "No" to these issues and has given reasons for its answer that will find acceptance in the minds of the audience and of the judges, it has won the debate. It is easy, then, to see why "determining the issues," and showing the audience what these issues are, is the second step in successful debating.

Although there is no fixed rule or touchstone by which an issue can immediately be determined, there are several rules which will aid in finding them.

1. In all your thinking and reading upon the question, constantly try to decide: (1) What will the other side admit? (2) Is there anything that I am thinking of in connection with this question that is not essential to it?

2. Do not try to make a final determination of the issues until you are sure you understand the question.

3. Be always ready to change your issues when you see that they are not fundamental.

With these general rules in mind, think the question over carefully. This process of determining the issues can, and should, go on at the same time as the process of learning what the question means. One helps the other. Having decided what will be the issues of the debate, set those issues down under appropriate heads; such as, "Is desirable," "Is needed," "Would work well," etc. Whenever you think of a reason why a thing is not needed, would not work, etc., put that down in a similar way. Now read more carefully (see "Reading References," Appendix I) on both sides of the question, and, whenever you find a reason for or against the proposition, set it down as above. The best method of doing this is to have a small pack of plain cards, perhaps two and one-half by four inches. Use one for each reason that you put down. As you think and read you will determine many reasons for the truth or falsity of the proposition. Gradually you will see that a great many of them are not so important as others and that they do not bear directly on the question, but in reality support some more important reason that you have set down. As you begin to notice this, go through your pack of cards and arrange them in the order of importance. Begin a new pile with every statement that seems to bear directly upon the proposition and put under it those statements that seem to support it. You will soon find that you have all your cards in two or three piles. Now examine the cards which you have on the top of each pile. See if the proof of these statements would convince any person that you are right. If so you have probably found the issues.

Always think first, then read, then think again.

If you have determined the issues wisely, it will be easy in the debate itself to show the audience and the judges what those issues are. You will have a tremendous advantage over your opponent, who in his haste or laziness may have chosen what are not the real issues of the question. He may present well the material that he has, but if that material does not support the *fundamental issues* of the question, you are right in calling the attention of the judges to that fact.

Few debates are won on the platform. They are won by thoughtful preparation. Be prepared.

SUGGESTED EXERCISES

1. Give in your own words, as briefly as you can, a definition of the term "the issues of a question."

2. Give one illustration of your own of the issues of a question.

3. What is meant by "determining the issues"?

4. Will the affirmative and the negative teams always agree on the issues?

5. Can a question have two entirely different sets of issues? Why, or why not?

6. If there can be only one correct set of issues for a question, and you believe that you have determined those, what must you do in the debate if your opponents advance different issues?

7. Think over carefully and set down what you believe are the issues of one of the following propositions. Frame the issues as questions.

(1) *a)* Football Should Be Abolished in This [your own] School.

b) Football Should Be Installed as a Regular Branch of Athletics in This [your own] School.

(2) *a*) Manual Training $\left\{\begin{array}{l}\text{Should Be Established in This}\\ \text{[your own] School.}\end{array}\right.$
Domestic Science

b) Manual Training $\left\{\text{For}\left\{\begin{array}{l}\text{Boys} \left\{\text{Should Be Made Com-}\right.\\ \text{Girls} \left\{\text{pulsory in This [your}\right.\end{array}\right.\right.$
Domestic Science
own] School.

8. Are there any terms in any of the above propositions which should be made more clear to an average audience? Are there any terms on the meaning of which two opposing teams might disagree?

9. Define one such term so that it would be clear and convincing to an audience not connected with the school.

10. Give two reasons why you believe it is or is not beneficial to study argumentation and debating.

11. If you were debating the question, "This [your own school] Should Establish a School Lunch-Room," would you take as one of the issues, "All students could obtain a warm meal at noon." Why, or why not?

LESSON V

HOW TO PROVE THE ISSUES

I. What "proof" is.
II. A consideration of how "proof" of anything is accomplished.
III. An infallible test of what the audience will believe.
IV. The material of proof-evidence.
V. Evidence and proof compared.

Having determined what the issues are, and having shown the audience why the establishment of these issues should logically win belief in your proposition, all that remains is to prove the issues.

Now it is clear that neither the audience nor the judges can be led to agree with us and to accept our issues as proved, by our telling them that we should like to have them believe in the soundness of our views. Neither can we succeed in convincing them by telling them that they ought to believe as we wish. The modern audience is not to be cajoled or browbeaten into belief. How, then, are we to persuade our hearers to accept our assertions as true? The only method is to give them what they demand—reasons. We must tell *why* every statement is true. This process of telling why the issues are true so effectively that the audience and judges believe them to be true is called the *proof*.

27

Naturally, the reasons that we give in support
of the issues will be no better than the issues themselves, unless we know what reasons the audience
will believe. And how are we to know what
reasons the audience will believe? We can best
answer that question by determining why we
ourselves believe those things which we accept.
Why do we believe anything? We believe that
water is wet; the sky, blue; fire, hot; and sugar,
sweet, because in our *experience* we have always
found them so. These things we believe because
we have *experienced* them ourselves. There are
other things that we believe in a similar way.
We believe that not every newspaper report is
reliable. We believe that a statement in the *Outlook*, the *Review of Reviews*, or the *World's Work*
is likely to be more trustworthy than a yellow
headline in the *Morning Bugle*. Our own experience, plus what we have heard of the experience of
others, has led us to this belief. But there are still
other things that we believe although we have not
experienced them at all. We believe that Columbus visited America in 1492, that Grant was a great
general, that Washington was our first president.
Directly, these things have never been experienced
by us, but indirectly they have. Others, within
whose experience these things have fallen, have led
us to accept them so thoroughly that they have
become our experience second hand.

If we are told that a man who was in the Iroquois
Theater fire was seriously burned, it seems reason-

able to us because our experience recognizes
burning as the result of such a situation. But if
we are told that a man who fell into the water
emerged dry, or that a general who served under
Washington was born in 1830, we discredit it
because such statements are not in accord with our
experience. We are ready, then, to answer our
question: *"What reasons will those in the audience
believe?" They will believe those statements which
harmonize with their own experience, and will discredit those which are at variance with their experience.* This experience, as we have seen, may be
first hand, or direct; or it may be indirect, or
second hand.

In every case, the speaker's argument must
base every issue upon reasons that rest on what
the hearers believe because of their own direct
or indirect experience. Suppose I assert: "John
Quinn was a dangerous man." Someone says:
"Prove that statement." I answer: "He was
a thief." Someone says: "If that is true, he
was a bad man, but can you prove him a thief?"
Then I produce a copy of a court record which
states that, on a certain day, a duly constituted court found John Quinn guilty of robbing
a bank. All my hearers now admit, not only
that he was a thief, but also that he was a
dangerous person. I have given them a reason
for my statement, and a reason for that reason,
until at last I have shown them that my assertion, that John Quinn is a dangerous citizen, rests

on what they themselves believe—that a court record is reliable.

Sometimes an issue cannot be supported by a reason that will come at once within the experience of the audience. It is then necessary to support the first by a second reason that does come within its experience. Remember, then, as the fundamental rule, that the judges and audience will believe the issues of the proposition, and, as a result, the proposition itself, only when we show them, by the standard of their own experience, that we are right.

The reasons that we give in support of the issues are, in debating, called *evidence*. Evidence is not proof; evidence is the material out of which proof is made. Evidence is like the separate stones of a solid wall: no one alone makes the wall; each one helps make it strong. Evidence is like the small rods and braces of the truss bridge: no one alone supports the weight; each helps to sustain the great beams that are the real support of the bridge.

Suppose we had the proposition: "The Honor System of Examinations Should Be Established in the Greenburg High School." We assert: "There is but one issue: Will the students be honest in the examination?" Now, what evidence shall we use to show that they will be honest? We may turn to the experience of other schools. After a careful investigation we find evidence with which we may support the assertion in the following way:

The Honor System should be established in the Greenburg High School, for:

I. The student will do honest work under that system, for:
   1. Experience of similar schools shows this, for:
      (1) This plan was a success in X High School, for:
         a) The principal of that school states [quotation from principal], for:
            (a) See *School Review*, Mar., 1900.
      (2) This plan is approved by Y High School, for:
         a) Etc.

Here the statements used in support of the issue are evidence. If the evidence is strong enough to bring conviction to the audience to which you are speaking, it is proof.

But notice here an important point. Why should this tend to make those in the audience believe that the honor system should be adopted? Simply because we have shown them that it has worked well elsewhere, and *their own experience tells them that what has been a benefit in other schools similar to this will be a benefit here.*

And in its final analysis this evidence is no stronger than the words of the men who state that it has worked in schools (X) and (Y).

If the experience of the audience is that these men are untruthful or likely to exaggerate, our evidence will not be good evidence. If the experience of the audience is that these men are capable, honest, and reliable, this evidence will go far toward gaining acceptance of, and belief in, our proposition.

Many attempts have been made to put evidence into different classes and to give tests of good evidence. There is but one rule that the debater needs to use: *In judging evidence for a debate consider what the effect will be on the audience and the judges. Will it be convincing to them?* In other words, will it make their own experience quickly and strongly support the issues?

Time is always limited in a debate. The wise debater will then choose that evidence which will most quickly make his hearers feel that their own experience proves him right. When the speaker has done this, he has chosen the best evidence and has used enough of it.

In courts of law where witnesses appear in every case and testify as to circumstances that did or did not occur, it is necessary that the jury be able to distinguish carefully between what it should and should not believe. Witnesses often have a keen personal interest in the verdict and, therefore, are inclined to tell less or more than the truth. Sometimes witnesses are relatives of persons who would suffer if the case were decided against them and they have a tendency to give unfair testimony.

In order that the jury may decide as fairly as possible what evidence is sound and what is not, the attorneys on each side of the case make out a copy of what are called instructions. These are given to the judge who, provided he approves of them, reads them to the jury. Usually these instructions urge the jurors to consider four things. They must consider, first, whether or not the statements of the witness are probable; that is, are they consistent with human experience? Do they seem reasonable and natural? A second thing which the jury is told to bear in mind is the opportunity which the witness had of observing the facts of which he speaks. Was he in a position to be familiar with the thing he describes? In this connection, the jury is sometimes instructed to consider the physical and mental qualities of the witness. Is he a man who is physically and mentally able to judge what he observes under such circumstances? A third factor which the jury must consider is the possibility of prejudice on the part of the witness. Has he any reason to feel more favorably toward one side than toward the other? Is the defendant his friend or relative or employer? A final consideration is what is commonly called "interest in the case." It is clear that if the witness will be benefited by a certain verdict, he may be inclined to frame his evidence in such a way that it will tend toward that verdict. All these considerations are based on the rule of referring to experience. What a judge really says in a charge to the jury is this: "Does your experience warn you that the testimony of some of these witnesses is unsound? Determine upon that basis in what respects these witnesses have told the whole truth and in what respects they have not."

To summarize: The issues of a proposition are proved by being supported with evidence. Since evidence is the material with which we build the connection between the issues and the experience of the audience, that evidence will be best which will receive the quickest and strongest support from the experience of the hearers.[1]

SUGGESTED EXERCISES

1. In the following extract from a speech of Burke, the famous debater has asserted that it is undesirable to use force upon the American colonies. State the four main reasons why he thinks so. Under each principal reason, put the reasons or evidence with which it is supported. Is this evidence convincing? Why, or why not?

First, Sir, permit me to observe that the use of force alone is but temporary. It may subdue for a moment, but it does not remove the necessity of subduing again; and a nation is not governed which is perpetually to be conquered.

My next objection is its uncertainty. Terror is not always the effect of force, and an armament is not a victory. If you do not succeed, you are without resource; for, conciliation failing, force remains; but, force failing, no further hope of reconciliation is left. Power and authority are sometimes bought by kindness; but they can never be begged as alms by an impoverished and defeated violence.

A further objection to force is that you impair the object by your very endeavor to preserve it. The thing you fought for is not the thing which you recover; but depreciated, sunk, wasted, and consumed in the contest. Nothing less will content me than whole America. I do not choose to consume its strength along with our own, because in all parts it is the British strength that I consume. I do not choose to be caught by a foreign enemy at the end of this exhausting conflict; and still less in the midst of it. I may escape; but I can make no insurance against such an event. Let me add that I do not choose wholly to break the American spirit; because it is the spirit that has made the country.

Lastly, we have no sort of experience in favor of force as an instrument in the rule of our Colonies. Their growth and their utility has been owing to methods altogether different. Our

[1] For a thorough discussion of the principle of reference to experience, see Arthur E. Phillips, *Effective Speaking*, chap. iii.

ancient indulgence has been said to be pursued to a fault. It may be so. But we know, if feeling is evidence, that our fault was more tolerable than our attempt to mend it; and our sin far more salutary than our penitence.

2. Wells's *Geometry* gives the following proposition: "Two perpendiculars to the same straight line are parallel." The evidence given is: "If they are not parallel, they will, if sufficiently produced, meet at some point, which is impossible, because from a given point without a straight line but one perpendicular can be drawn." Is this evidence sufficient to constitute proof? Does it convince you? Why, or why not?

3. Set down as much evidence as you can think of in ten minutes, to convince a business man that a high-school education is an advantage in business life.

4. Support the statement that football has benefited or harmed this school, with five truthful statements that are evidence. Indicate which ones would be most effective, if you were speaking to the students, and which would make the strongest impression on the faculty.

5. In the following statements of testimony, tell which ones would be good evidence and which not. Tell why or why not in each case.

(1) X, a student, was told that unless he should point out the pupil who had put matches on the floor, he would be expelled. X then said that Y was guilty.

(2) James Brown, a teamster, asserts that the use of alcohol is beneficial to all persons.

(3) John Burns, a labor leader, declares that labor unions are beneficial to trade.

(4) F. W. McCorkle, a large manufacturer, states that labor unions have proved beneficial to commerce.

(5) Professor Sheldon, a college president and profound student of economics, has declared that labor unions help the trade of the world.

(6) Henry Hawkins, a student at the Johnstown High School, asserts that they have the best football team in the state.

(7) M. Metchnikoff, chief attendant at the Pasteur Institute, says: "As for myself, I am convinced that alcohol is a poison." M. Berthelot, member of the Academy of Science and Medicine, states: "Alcohol is not a food, even though it may be a fuel."

(8) Lord Chatham, a member of the English Parliament, said, in speaking of the Revolutionary War: "It is a struggle of free and virtuous patriots."

6. On the basis of your answers to 5, state three conditions that would make a man's speaking or writing weak evidence as testimony; three that would make a man's testimony strong.

7. In Exercise 5 is (3), (4), or (5) the strongest testimony in favor of labor unions. Why? Which is next?

8. Can you see one danger of relying on testimony alone for evidence?

LESSON VI

THE BRIEF. THE CHOICE AND USE OF EVIDENCE

I. What the brief is.

II. What the brief does.

III. Parts of the brief:
1. The introduction in which—
   (1) The end desired is made clear.
   (2) The issues are determined.
2. The proof, which states the issues as facts and proves them.
3. The conclusion, which is a formal summary of the proof.

IV. A specimen model brief.

V. A specimen special brief.

VI. Rules for briefing.

When a builder begins the construction of a wall, he must have the proper material at hand. When an engineer begins the construction of a steel bridge, he must have metal of the right forms and shapes. Neither of these men, however, can accomplish the end which he has in mind unless he takes this material and puts it together in the proper way. So it is with the debater. He may have plenty of good evidence, but he will never win unless that evidence is organized, that is, put together in the most effective manner.

The builder, if he were building a wall of concrete, would get the correct form by pouring the concrete into a mold. So also, there is a mold

which the debater should use in shaping his
evidence. When the evidence has been put into
this form, the debater is said to have constructed
a *brief*.

In a previous lesson we saw how we might prove
that John Quinn was a dangerous man by using
the evidence of a court record. If we had put
that evidence in brief-form we should have had
this:

John Quinn was a dangerous man, for:
1. He was a thief, for:
    (1) The Illinois state courts found him guilty of robbing
       a bank, for:
       a) See *Ill. Court Reports*, Vol. X., p. 83.

The brief, then, is a concise, logical outline of
everything that the speaker wishes to say to the
audience.

Its purpose is to indicate in the most definite
form every step through which the hearers must
be taken in order that the proposition may at
last be fully accepted by their experience.

The brief is for the debater himself. He does
not show it to the audience. It is the framework
of his argument. It is the path which, if carefully
marked out, will lead to success.

Now, as we have seen, there are three principal
steps in debating:

1. Making clear what you wish the audience to
believe.

2. Showing the audience why the establishing of
certain issues should make them believe this.

3. Proving these issues.

The first two of these steps constitute what in the brief is called the *Introduction*.

The third step, proving the issues, is the largest part of the brief and is called the *Body* or the *Proof*.

In addition to these two divisions of the brief there is a sort of formal summary at the end called the *Conclusion*.

The skeleton of a brief then would be as follows:

INTRODUCTION

In which: (1) the desired end is made clear; (2) the issues are determined.

PROOF

In which the issues are stated as declarations or assertions and definite reasons are given why each one should be believed. These reasons are in turn supported by other reasons until the assertion is finally brought within the hearers' experience.

CONCLUSION

In which the proof is summarized.

Of course no two briefs are identical, but all must follow this general plan. Suppose we look at what might be called a model brief.

MODEL BRIEF

Statement of proposition.

INTRODUCTION

   I. Definition of terms.
  II. Restatement of question in light of these terms.
 III. Determination of issues.
       1. Statement of what both sides admit.
       2. Statement of what is irrelevant.
  IV. Statement of the issues.

PROOF

I. The first issue is true, for:
    1. This reason, which is true, for:
        (1) This reason, for:
            a) This reason.
            b) This reason.
    2. This reason, for:
        (1) This evidence.
        (2) This authority.
        (3) This testimony, for:
            a) See Vol. X, p. –, of report, document, magazine, or book.
II. The second issue is true, for:
    1. This reason, for:
        (1) This reason.
    2. This reason, for:
        (1) This reason.
        (2) This reason.
III. The third issue is true, for:
    1. This reason, etc.
IV. The fourth issue is true, for:
    1. This reason, etc.

CONCLUSION

Therefore, since we have shown: (1) that the first issue is true by this evidence; (2) that the second issue is well founded by this evidence; (3) that the third and fourth, etc.; we conclude that our proposition is true.

Now, let us look at a special brief, made out in a high-school debate, for a special subject.

The preceding is an affirmative brief and there were four issues. In the following we have a negative brief, in which there were three issues. Refutation is introduced near the close of the proof.

Of this we shall see more in the next lesson.

BRIEF FOR NEGATIVE

INTRA-HIGH-SCHOOL CONTESTS SHOULD BE SUBSTITUTED
FOR INTER-HIGH-SCHOOL CONTESTS IN THE
HIGH SCHOOLS OF NORTHERN ILLINOIS

INTRODUCTION

I. Definition of terms.
  1. Contests, ordinary competitions in:
     a) Athletics.
     b) Debating.
  2. Intra-high-school contests (contests within each school).
  3. Inter-high-school contests (contests between different high schools).

II. Restatement of question in light of these definitions. Contests within each high school should be substituted for contests between high schools in Northern Illinois.

III. Determination of issues.
  1. It is admitted that:
     a) Inter and intra contests both exist at present in the high schools of Northern Illinois.
     b) Contest work is a desirable form of training.
     c) Not all contests should be abolished.
  2. Certain educators have asserted that:
     a) The inter form of contests is open to abuses.
     b) The intra contests would be more democratic.
     c) Intra contests would be practicable.
  3. Other educators disagree with these assertions.
  4. The issues, then, are:
     a) Are the inter contests so widely abused in the high schools of Northern Illinois as to warrant their abolition?
     b) Would the proposed plan be more democratic than the present system?
     c) Would the proposed plan work out in practice?

PROOF

I. Contests between the high schools of Northern Illinois are not subject to such abuses as will warrant their abolition, for:

  A. If the abuses alleged against athletic contests ever existed, they are now extinct, for:

    1. The alleged danger of injury to players physically unfit is not an existing danger, for:

      (1) It has been made impossible by the rules of the schools, for:

        a) This high school requires a physician's certificate of fitness before participation in any athletic contest, for:

          (*a*) Extract from athletic rulings of school board.

        b) Our opponent's high school has a similar regulation, for:

          (*a*) Extract from school paper of opponents.

        c) The X High School has the same ruling.

        d) The Y High School has the same requirement.

    2. The charge that athletic contests between high schools make the contestants poor students is without sound basis, for:

      (1) A high standard of scholarship is required of all inter-high-school athletic contestants, for:

        a) Regulations of Illinois Athletic Association.

  B. The evils charged against inter-high-school debating cannot be cured by the proposed scheme, for:

    1. They are due, when they exist, not to the form of contest, but to improper coaching, for:

      (1) "Too much training," one of the evils charged, is an example of this.

      (2) Unfair use of evidence, the other evil alleged, is simply an evil of improper coaching.

II. The proposed plan would not be so democratic as the present system, for:

  A. The present plan gives an opportunity to all students, for:

    1. Its class and other intra contests give a chance to the less proficient pupils.

    2. Its inter contests afford an opportunity for the more proficient pupils.

  B. The proposed plan would deprive the more capable pupils of desirable contests, for:

    1. They can find contests strenuous enough to induce development only by competing with similar students in other schools.

III. The proposed plan would not be practicable, for:

  A. It is unsound in theory, for:

    1. No pupil has a strong desire to defeat his close friends.

    2. There is no desirable method of dividing the students for competition under the proposed plan, for:

      (1) Class division is unsatisfactory, for:

        a) The more mature and experienced upper classes win too easily.

      (2) "Group division" is not desirable, for:

        a) If the division is large, the domination of the mature students will give no opportunity to the younger students.

        b) If the division is small, it is likely to develop into a secret society.

  B. Experience opposes the proposed plan, for:

    1. College experience is against it, for:

      (1) N. University tried this plan without success, for:

        a) Quotation from president of N.

2. High-school experience does not indorse it, for:
(1) It is practically untried in high schools.

REFUTATION

I. The argument which the affirmative may advance, that the experience of Shortridge High School demonstrates the success of this plan, is without weight, for:

A. It is not applicable to this question, for:
1. The plan at Shortridge is not identical with the proposed plan, for:
(1) Shortridge has not entirely abolished inter contests, for:
a) School Review, October, 1911.
2. Conditions in Shortridge differ from those in the high schools of Northern Illinois, for:
(1) Faculty of that school has unusual efficiency in coaching, for:
a) Extract from letter of principal.
(2) Larger number of students, for:
a) Extract from letter of principal.

CONCLUSION

Since there is no opportunity for serious abuse arising from contests between schools, and since the adoption of contests within the schools alone would lessen the democracy of contests as a form of education, and since the proposed plan is impracticable in theory and has never been put into successful operation, the negative concludes that the substitution of intra for inter contests is not desirable in the high schools of Northern Illinois.

From these illustrative briefs we can draw:

RULES FOR BRIEFING

The introduction should contain only such material as both sides will admit, or, as you can show, should reasonably admit, from the phrasing of the proposition.

Scrupulous care should be used in the numbering and lettering of all statements and substatements.

Each issue should be a logical reason for the truth of the proposition.

Each substatement should be a logical reason for the issue or statement that it supports.

Each issue in the proof and each statement that has supporting statements should be followed by the word "for."

Each reason given in support of the issues and each subreason should be no more than a simple, complete, declarative sentence.

The word "for" should never appear as a connective between a statement and substatement in the introduction.

The words "hence" and "therefore" should never appear in the proof of the brief, but one should be able to read *up* through the brief and by substituting the word "therefore" for the word "for" in each case, arrive at the proposition as a conclusion.

Suggested Exercises

1. Turn to Exercise 1, in Lesson V, and carefully brief the selection from Burke.

2. Is the following extract from a high-school student's brief correct in form? Criticize it in regard to arrangement of ideas, and correct it so far as is possible without using new material.

SOCCER FOOTBALL SHOULD BE ADOPTED IN THE "A" HIGH
SCHOOL AS A REGULAR BRANCH OF ATHLETIC SPORT

INTRODUCTION

I. Recent popularity of soccer.
    1. In England.
    2. In America.
II. Soccer a healthful game, for:
    1. Develops lungs.
    2. Develops all the muscles.
III. Issues.
    1. Soccer is a beneficial game.
    2. Would the students of "A" support soccer as a regular
       sport?

PROOF

I. Soccer is a beneficial sport, for:
    1. It requires much running, kicking, and dodging, both
       in offensive and defensive playing, therefore—
       (1) It develops muscles.
       (2) It develops lungs.
    2. It is played out of doors, therefore
       (1) It develops lungs.
II. Students of "A" would support soccer as a regular sport, for:
    1. Who has ever heard of students who would not support
       soccer, baseball, basket-ball, and all other exciting
       games?

3. The following is the conclusion of an argument by
Edmund Burke in which the speaker maintained that
Warren Hastings should be impeached by the House of
Commons. If it had been preceded by a clear "intro-
duction" and convincing "proof," do you think that it
would have made an effective "conclusion"?

Therefore, it is with confidence that, ordered by the Commons:
I impeach Warren Hastings, Esquire, of high crimes and
misdemeanors.
I impeach him in the name of the Commons of Great Britain,
in Parliament assembled, whose parliamentary trust he has
betrayed.

I impeach him in the name of all the Commons of Great Britain, whose national character he has dishonored.

I impeach him in the name of the people of India, whose laws, rights, and liberties he has subverted, whose property he has destroyed, whose country he has laid waste and desolate.

I impeach him in the name and by virtue of those eternal laws of justice which he has violated.

I impeach him in the name of human nature itself, which he has cruelly outraged, injured, and oppressed in both sexes, in every age, rank, situation, and condition of life.

4. Take any one of the following propositions and without other material than that of your own ideas, state at least two issues, and, in correct brief form, proof for belief or unbelief.

(1) High-School Boys Should Smoke Cigarettes.

(2) No One Should Play Football without a Physician's Permission.

(3) Girls Should Participate in Athletic Games While in High School.

(4) High-School Fraternities Are Desirable.

(5) Women Should Have the Right to Vote in All Elections.

LESSON VII

THE FORENSIC

I. What the forensic is.
II. How the forensic may be developed and delivered:
    1. By writing and reading from manuscript:
        (1) Advantages and disadvantages.
    2. By writing and committing to memory:
        (1) Advantages and disadvantages.
    3. By oral development from the brief:
        (1) Advantages.
III. Style and gestures in the delivery of the forensic.

When the brief is finished, the material is ready to be put into its final form. This final form is called the *forensic*.

As practically all debates are conducted by means of teams, the work of preparing the forensic is usually divided among the members of the team. The brief may be divided in any way, but it is desirable that each member of the team should have one complete, logical division. So it often happens that each member of the team develops one issue into its final form.

The forensic is nothing but a rounding-out of the brief. The brief is a skeleton: the forensic is that skeleton developed into a complete literary form. Into this form the oral delivery breathes the spirit of living ideas.

No better illustration of the brief expanded into the full forensic need be given than that in Exercise

1, Lesson V. Compare the brief which you made of this extract from Burke with the forensic itself, a few paragraphs of which are quoted there. Any student will find that merely to glance through a part of this speech of Burke's is an excellent lesson in brief-making and in the production of forensics. First study the skeleton only—the brief—by reading the opening sentences of each paragraph. Then see how this skeleton is built into a forensic by the splendid rhetoric of the great British statesman.[1]

There are two ways in which the forensic may be developed from the brief. Both have some advantages, varying with the conditions of the debate. One is to write out every word of the forensic. When this is done, the debater may, if he wishes, read from his manuscript to the audience. If he does so, his chances of making a marked effect are little better than if he spoke from the bottom of a well. The average audience will not follow the speaker who is occupied with raveling ideas from his paper rather than with weaving them into the minds of his hearers.

The debater who writes his forensic may, however, learn it and deliver it from memory. This method has some decided advantages. In every debate the time is limited; and by writing and rewriting the ideas can be compressed into their briefest and most definite form. Besides, the speaker may practice upon this definite forensic to determine the rapidity with which he must speak

[1] Edmund Burke, *On Conciliation with the Colonies.*

in order to finish his argument in the allotted time.

At the same time this plan has several unfavorable aspects. When the debater has prepared himself in this way, forgetting is fatal. He has memorized words. When the words do not come he has no recourse but to wait for memory to revive, or to look to his colleagues for help. Again, the man who has learned his argument can give no variety to his attack or defense. He is like a general with an immovable battery, who, though able to hurl a terrific discharge in the one direction in which his guns point, is powerless if the attack is made ever so slightly on his flank. Perhaps the greatest disadvantage of this method is that it does not give the student the best kind of training. What he needs most in life is the ability to arrange and present ideas rapidly, not to speak a part by rote.

It would seem, then, that this plan should be advised only when the students are working for one formal debate, and are not preparing for a series of class or local contests that can all be controlled by the same instructor or critic. With beginners in oral argumentation this method will usually make the better showing, and may therefore be considered permissible in the case of those teams which, because of unfamiliarity with their opponents' methods, can take no chances. This plan of preparation is in no way harmful or dishonest, but lacks some of the more permanent advantages of the second method.

The second method of developing the brief into the forensic is by *oral composition*. This method demands that the debater shall *speak extemporaneously* from his *memorized brief*. This in no way means that careful preparation, deliberate thought, and precise organization are omitted. On the contrary, the formation of a brief from which a winning forensic can be expanded requires the most studious preparation, the keenest thought, and the most careful organization. Neither does it mean that, as soon as the brief is formed, the forensic can be presented. Before that step is taken, the debater who will be successful will spend much time, not in *written*, but in *oral* composition.

He will study his brief until he sees that it is not merely a succession of formal statements connected with "for's," but a series of ideas arranged in that form because they will, if presented in that order, bring conviction to his hearers. "Learning the brief," then, becomes not a case of memory, but a matter of seeing—seeing what comes next because that is the only thing that logically could come next. When the brief is in mind, the speaker will expand it into a forensic to an imaginary audience until he finds that he is expressing the ideas clearly, smoothly, and readily. Pay no attention to the fact that in the course of repeated deliveries the words will vary. Words make little difference if the framework of ideas is the same.

This method of composing the forensic trains
the mind of the student to see the logical relation-
ship of ideas, to acquire a command of language,
and to vary the order of ideas if necessary. In
doing these things, there are developed those
qualities that are essential to all effective speaking.

A debater's success in giving unity and coherence
to his argument depends chiefly on his method of
introducing new ideas in supporting his issues.
These changes from one idea to another, or transitions, as they are called, should always be made so
that the hearer's attention will be recalled to the
assertion which the new idea is intended to support.
Suppose we have made this assertion: "Contests
within schools are more desirable than contests
between schools." We are planning to support
this by proving: first, that the contests between
schools are very much abused; second, that the
proposed plan will be more democratic; and third,
that the proposed plan will work well in practice.
In supporting these issues, we should, of course,
present a great deal of material. When we are
ready to change from the first supporting idea
to the second, we must make that change in such
a way that our hearers will know that we are
planning to prove the second main point of our
contention. But this is not enough. We must
make that change so that they will be definitely
reminded of what we have already proved. The
same thing will hold true when we change to the
third contention.

The following illustrates a faulty method of transition: Contests between schools are so abused that they should be abolished [followed by all the supporting material]. The proposed plan will be more democratic than the present [followed by its support]. The proposed plan would work well in practice [followed by its support]. No matter how thoroughly we might prove each of these, they would impress the audience as standing alone; they would show no coherence, no connection with one another. The following would be a better method: Contests within schools should be substituted for those between schools because contests between schools are open to abuses so great as to warrant their abolition [followed by its support]. We should then begin to prove the second issue in this way: But not only are contests between schools so open to abuse that they should be abolished, but they are less desirable than contests within schools for they are less democratic. [This will then be followed with the support of the second issue.] The transition to the third issue should be made in this way: Now, honorable judges, we have shown you that contests between schools are not worthy of continuance; we have shown you that the plan which we propose will be better in its democracy than the system at present in vogue; we now propose to complete our argument by showing you that our plan will work well in practice. [This would then be followed with the proper supporting material.]

Great speakers have shown that they realized the importance of these cementing transitions. Take for example Burke's argument that force will be an undesirable instrument to use against the colonies. He says: "First, permit me to observe that the use of force shall be temporary." The next paragraph he begins: "My next observation is its uncertainty." He follows that with: "A further observation to force is that you impair the object by your very endeavor to preserve it." And he concludes: "Lastly, we have no sort of experience in favor of force as an instrument in the rule of our colonies." He used this principle to perhaps even greater advantage when he argued that "a fierce spirit of liberty had grown up in the colonies." He supports this with claims which are introduced as follows:

"First, the people of the colonies are descendants of Englishmen."

"They were further confirmed in this pleasing error [their spirit of liberty] by the form of their provincial legislative assemblies."

"If anything were wanting to this necessary operation of the form of government, religion would have given it a complete effect."

"There is, in the South, a circumstance attending these colonies which, in my opinion, fully counterbalances this difference, and makes the spirit of liberty still more high and haughty than in those to the northward. It is that in Virginia and the Carolinas, they have a vast multitude of slaves."

"Permit me, Sir, to add another circumstance in our colonies, which contributes no mean part towards the growth and effect of this untractable spirit. I mean their education."

"The last cause of this disobedient spirit in the colonies is hardly less powerful than the rest as it is not merely moral, but laid deep in the natural constitution of things. Three thousand miles of ocean lie between you and them."

He finally summarizes these in this way, which further ties them together.

"Then, Sir, from these six capital sources; of descent; of form of government; of religion in the northern provinces; of manners in the southern; of education; of the remoteness of situation from the first mover of government; from all these causes a fierce spirit of liberty has grown up."

It may be well also to point out more clearly the somewhat special nature of the first speeches on each side. The first speech of the affirmative must, of course, make clear to the judges and the audience what you wish them to believe. This will involve all the steps which have already been pointed out as necessary to accomplish that result. The first speaker can gain a great deal for his side by presenting this material not only with great clearness, but in a manner which will win the good-will of the audience toward himself, his team, and his side of the subject. To do this, he must be genial, honest, modest, and fair. He must make his hearers feel that he is not giving a narrow or prejudiced analysis of the question; he must make them feel that his treatment is open and fair to both sides, and that he finally reaches the issues not at all because he *wishes* to find those issues, but because a thorough analysis of the question will allow him to reach no others.

The first speaker on the negative side may have much the same work to do. If, however, he agrees with what the first speaker of the affirmative has said, he will save time merely by stating that fact and by summarizing in a sentence or two the steps leading to the issues. If he does not agree with the interpretation which the affirmative has given to the question, it will be necessary for him to interpret the question himself. He must make clear to the judges why his analysis is correct and that of his opponent faulty.

In presenting the forensic to the judges and audience forget, so far as possible, that you are debating. You have a proposition in which you believe and which you want them to accept. Your purpose is not to make your hearers say: "How well he does it." You want them to say: "He is right."

Do not rant. Speak clearly, that you may be understood; and with enough force that you may be heard, but in the same manner that you use in conversation.

Good gestures help. *Good gestures* are those that come naturally in support of your ideas. While practicing alone notice what gestures you put in involuntarily. They are right. Do not ape anyone in gesture. Your oral work will be more effective without use of your hands than it will be with an ineffective use of them. The most ineffective use is the making of motions that are so violent or extravagant that they attract the listeners' attention to themselves and away from your ideas. Remember that the expression of your face is most important of all gestures. Earnest interest, pleasantness, fairness, and vigor expressed in the speaker's face at the right times have done more to win debates than other gestures have ever accomplished.

LESSON VIII

REFUTATION

I. Refutation explained.

II. Refutation may be carried on:
1. By overwhelming constructive argument.
2. By showing the weakness of opponents' argument.

III. The time for refutation:
1. Allotted time.
2. Special times.

IV. The right spirit in refutation.

Our work up to this point has dealt with what is called the *constructive argument*, i.e., the building up of the proof. But to make the judges believe as you wish, you must not merely support your contentions; you must destroy the proof which your opponents are trying to construct.

As with the successful athletic team and the successful general, so with the successful debater, it is necessary, not only to attack, but also to repulse; not only to carry out the plan of your own side, but to meet and defeat the plan which the other side has developed. In debating, this repulse, this destruction of the arguments of the opposition, is called *refutation* or *rebuttal*.

There are two principal ways in which the refutation of the opponent's argument can be accomplished. The first is *to destroy it with your own constructive argument.* The second is *to show that his argument, even though it is not destroyed by yours, is faulty in itself, and therefore useless.*

Although only one of them is labeled "Refutation" in the model brief in the sixth lesson, both types are illustrated there.

There the negative, believing that the first argument of the affirmative would be, "Inter contests are open to abuse," makes its first point a counter-assertion. It uses as the first issue: "Contests between the high schools of northern Illinois are not subject to such abuses as will warrant their abolition." Which side would gain this point in the minds of the judges would depend on which side supported its assertion with the better evidence.

If one side wished to raise this question again in the refutation speeches, which close the debate, it could do no better than to repeat and re-emphasize the same material which it used in its construction argument.

The second method of refuting, i.e., showing an argument to be faulty, is also illustrated in the brief in the sixth lesson. It is marked "Refutation." This material was introduced because the negative felt sure that the affirmative would attempt to use the experience of Shortridge High School as evidence of the successful working of this plan. It was shown to be faulty in that the experience of this school would not apply to the question here debated.

The student's study of what makes good evidence for his own case will enable him to see the weakness of his opponents' arguments. Apply the *same* tests to your opponents' evidence that you apply to your own. What is there about the evidence introduced that should make the audience hesitate to accept it? Point these things out to the audience. It may be that prejudiced, dishonest, or ignorant testimony has been given. It may be that not enough evidence has been given to carry weight. Whatever the flaw, point out to the audience that, upon a critical examination, experience shows the evidence to be weak.

In every debate there is a regular time allowed for rebuttal. This is, however, not the only time at which it may be introduced. In the debate, put in refutation wherever it is needed. One of the best plans is, if possible, to refute with a few sentences at the opening of each speech what the previous speaker of the opposition has said.

In all refutation, *state clearly what you aim to disprove*. When quoting the statement of an opponent, be sure to be accurate.

Something like the following is a good form for stating refutation:

Our opponents, in arguing that labor unions have been harmful to the commerce of America, have stated that they would use as support the testimony of prominent men. In so doing, they have quoted from X, Y, and Z. This testimony is without strength. X, as a large employer of labor, would be open to prejudice; Y, as a non-union laborer, is both prejudiced and ignorant. The testimony of Z, as an Englishman is applicable to labor unions as they have affected, not the commerce of America, but the trade of England.

A similar form is shown in the brief on inter- and intra-high-school contests in refuting the experience of Shortridge High School.

In all refutation, keep close to the fundamental principles of the question. Do not be led astray into minute details upon which you differ. Never tire of recalling attention to the issues of the question. Show why those are the issues, and you will see that the strongest refutation almost always consists in pointing out wherein you have proved these issues, while your opponents have failed to do so.

In order to be fully prepared, however, it is a good plan to put upon cards all the points that your opponents may use and that you have not answered in your constructive argument. Adopt a method similar to this:

Shortridge argument
1. Will not apply for:
    (1) Not this plan.
    (2) Conditions differ, for:
        a) *School Review*, October, 1911.

Then if your opponents advance arguments that are not met in your speech, merely lay out these cards while they speak, and use them as references in your refutation.

The closing rebuttal speech is always a critical one. Here the speaker should again point out every mistake which his opponents have made.

If their interpretation of the question has been wrong, he should, while avoiding details, emphasize the chief flaws in their arguments. On the other hand, he should summarize the argument of his own side from beginning to end; he should make the support of each of the issues stand clearly before the judges in its complete, logical form.

In these closing speeches, as in the opening of the debate, much may be gained by an attitude which will win the favor of the hearers toward the speaker and his ideas. An attitude of petty criticism, of narrowness of view, is undesirable at any stage of the debate. The debater who is inclined to belittle his opponents will only belittle himself. To the judges it will appear that the speaker who has time to ridicule his adversaries must be a little short of arguments. Insinuations of dishonesty and attempts to be sarcastic should be carefully avoided. These weapons are sharp but they are two-edged and are more likely to injure the speaker than his opponent.

The right attitude for a debater is always one of fairness. Give your opponents all possible credit. When you have then refuted their arguments, your own contentions seem of double strength. It is said that Lincoln used this method with splendid effect: He would often restate the argument of his opponent with great force and clearness; he would make it seem irrefutable. Then, when he began his attack and caused his opponent's argument to collapse, its fall seemed to be utter and complete, while his arguments, which had proved themselves capable of effecting this destruction, appeared all the more powerful.

In your desire to do well in refutation, do not be led to depend upon that alone. There is no older and better rule than, "Know the other side as well as you know your own." Do not believe that this is in order that you may be ready with a clever answer for every point made by the other side. The most important reason why you should know the other side of the question is the necessity of your determining the issues correctly, and thus building a constructive argument that is overwhelming and impregnable. Many a debate has been lost because the debaters worked up their own constructive argument first, and only later, in order to prepare refutation, considered what their opponents would say. Had they proceeded correctly, they would have destroyed the proof of their adversaries while they built up their own.

A clever retort in refutation often wins the applause of the galleries, but an analysis of the question so keen that the real issues are determined, supported by an organization of evidence so strong that it sweeps away all opposition as it grows, is more likely to gain the favorable decision of the judges.

Suggested Exercises

1. What is the purpose of refutation?
2. What two principal methods may be followed?

3. What must one do to refute correctly and well?

4. Do you think it better in refutation to assail the minor points of your opponent or to attack the main issues?

5. A fellow-student in chemistry said to you: "The chemical symbol for water is H_4O; two of our classmates told me so." You replied: "The correct symbol, according to our instructor, is H_2O." Did you refute his assertion? How?

6. A classmate makes an argument which could be briefed thus:

Cigarettes are good for high-school boys, for:
1. They aid health of body, for:
   (1) Many athletes smoke them, for:
      a) X smokes them.
      b) Y smokes them.
      c) Z smokes them.

If you disagree with this assertion, do not believe they aid health, and know X does not smoke cigarettes, how would you refute his contention?

7. If your opponents in a debate quote opinions of others in support of their views, in what two ways can they be refuted?

8. In a recent campaign, the administration candidate used this argument: "I should be re-elected, for: Times are good, work is plentiful, crops are excellent, and products demand a high price." Show any weakness in this argument.

9. Show the weakness of proof in this argument:

Harvard is better at football than Princeton
1. They defeated Princeton in 1912.

10. What general rule can you make from 9 concerning a statement supported by particular cases?

LESSON IX

MANAGEMENT OF THE DEBATE

Teams.—The opposing teams in a debate usually consist of three persons each. A larger or smaller number is permissible.

Time of Speaking.—Each speaker is ordinarily allowed one constructive speech and one rebuttal speech. The constructive speech is usually about twice the length of the refutation. Twelve and six, ten and five, and eight and four minutes are all frequent time-limits for debates. Many debaters make shorter speeches.

Order of speaking.—The debate is opened by the affirmative. The first speaker is followed by a negative debater, who, in turn, is followed by a member of the affirmative team, and so on until the entire constructive argument is presented. A member of the negative team opens the refutation. Speakers then alternate until the debate is closed by the affirmative. The order of speakers on each team is often different in refutation than in constructive argument.

Presiding chairman.—Every debate should be presided over by a chairman. His duties are to state the question to the audience, introduce each speaker, and announce the decision of the judges. He sometimes also acts as timekeeper.

Timekeepers.—A timekeeper representing each of the competing organizations should note the moment when each speaker begins and notify the chair when the allotted time has been consumed. It is customary to give each speaker as many minutes of warning before his time expires as he may desire.

Salutation.—Good form in debating requires that each speaker shall begin with a salutation to the various personages whom he addresses. The most common salutation is: "Mr. Chairman, worthy opponents, honorable judges, ladies and gentlemen."

Reference to other speakers.—In referring to members of the opposing team never say, "he said," "she said," or "they said." Always speak of your opponents in the third person in some such way as, "my honorable opponents," "the first speaker of the negative," "the gentlemen of the affirmative," or "the gentlemen from X."

In referring to other members of your own team say, "my colleagues," or "my colleague, the first speaker," etc.

The judges.—There are generally three judges. Where it is practicable, a larger number is desirable because their opinion is more nearly the opinion of the audience as a whole. Needless to say they should be competent and wholly without prejudice as to teams or question.

The decision.—The decision of each judge should be written on a slip and sealed in an envelope provided for that purpose (see Appendix IX, "Forms for Judges' Decision"). These should be opened by the chairman in view of the audience, and the decision announced.

LESSON X

A SUMMARY AND A DIAGRAM

We have now completed our study of debating. We saw first that all talking and writing is discourse, and that one great division of discourse—that which aims to gain belief—is argumentation. Argumentation we divided into spoken and written argumentation. We found that it varies in formality but that, when carried on orally under prescribed conditions and with the expectation of having a decision rendered, it is called debating.

Successful debating we found to require three steps: showing the hearers what belief is desired; showing them upon what issues belief depends; and supporting these issues with evidence until we have established proof.

We learned that the first of these steps could be taken by stating the question in the form of a definite, single proposition; defining the terms of this proposition; and then restating the whole matter. We found that the second step required that the material that both sides admit, together with all other material that is really not pertinent to the question, should be first removed, and that the fundamentals of the question should be stated as the issues. The last step, proving the issues, we found to involve two processes. It was necessary, first, to find and select evidence, and, second, to arrange that evidence in logical order—the brief-form.

The accompanying diagram is one that has helped many students to visualize more clearly what is attempted in a debate and to see how the debate may be made successful.

The doubt that the audience very reasonably has of the new idea proposed is bridged over by the proposition. But this proposition will not be strong enough to cause the minds of the listeners to pass from unbelief to belief unless it is well supported. The whole proposition is therefore placed upon one or two or three great capitals— the issues, under each of which is a pillar of proof. These pillars are composed of evidence of every sort. The intelligent debater has, however, be-fore placing a single piece of this evdience in the proof, tested it carefully. He has tested it with the question: "Will it help bring conviction to the audience; how will it affect my hearers?" More-over, not satisfied with this scrupulous choice of evidence, he has been careful not to pile it in regard-less of position, but to place each piece in the posi-tion where it will lend the strongest support to the entire structure.

When this has been done, the bridge of proof is built solidly upon the experience of the hearers, and, almost without their knowledge, their minds have gone from unbelief to belief.

APPENDICES

APPENDIX I

HOW AND WHERE TO READ FOR MORE INFORMATION

Practically every subject that is interesting enough to be a good subject for debate has been written about by other people. Every good library contains the books on the following list, and with a little experience the student can handle them easily. A general treatment of every important subject can be found in any of the following encyclopedias: *Americana, New International, Twentieth Century, Britannica.*

Everything that has been written upon every subject in all general, technical, and school magazines, can be found by looking up the desired topic in: *The Reader's Guide to Periodical Literature*, or *Poole's Index.*

If the matter being studied deals with civics, economics, or sociology, look in: Bliss, *Encyclopaedia of Social Reform*, etc.; Lalor, *Cyclopaedia of Political Science*, etc.; Larned, *History of Ready Reference and Topical Reading;* Bowker and Iles, *Reader's Guide in Economics*, etc.

What Congress is doing and has done is often important. This can be found in full in: *The Congressional Record.*

Jones's *Finding List* tells where to look for any topic in various government publications.

In studying many subjects the need of definite and reliable statistics will be felt. These may be found on almost any question in the following publications: *Statesman's Yearbook, Whitaker's Almanac, World Almanac, Chicago Daily News Almanac, Hazell's Almanac, U.S. Census Reports.*

Never consider your reading completed until you have looked for any special book that may be written upon your subject in the Card Catalogue of your Library.

Make out a Bibliography or Reading List (as illustrated briefly in Appendix V) before you proceed to actual reading.

APPENDIX II

ILLUSTRATIONS OF ANALYSIS TO DETERMINE
THE ISSUES OF THE QUESTION

The two specimens that immediately follow are analyses of the same question by students of the same university. The first is a selection from the speech made by Mr. Raymond S. Pruitt in the Towle Debate of Northwestern University Law School in 1911. The second is the introduction to the speech made by Mr. Charles Watson of the Northwestern University Law School in the 1911 debate with the Law School of the University of Southern California. Students should observe how the two speakers determine somewhat different issues.

Resolved, That in actions against an employer for death or injury of an employee sustained in the course of an industrial employment the fellow-servant rule and the rule of the assumption of risk as defined and interpreted by the common law, should be abolished.

Mr. Pruitt, speaking for the affirmative:

The question which we discuss tonight is partly economic and partly legal. By that I mean that viewing it from the standpoint of legal liability, we possibly can agree with the gentlemen of the Negative that the employer should respond in damages to his injured employee, only when the injury has been caused by the employer's own fault. But, on the other hand, viewing the same problem from an economic standpoint, you cannot deny, that, when through no fault of his own, a worker is injured in the course of an industrial employment, that industry should compensate him for the loss.

Here then is the issue—the world-old-problem—established principles of law in conflict with changing social and economic conditions; and, as history shows, there can in such cases be but one solution. The decision of the court, the statute of the legislature, yes, even the constitution of the nation, must in turn yield to the march of progress and adapt itself to changing conditions until once more it shall reflect the sense of public justice in its own time. Hence, I say that in our discussion this evening, there can be no confusion of issues. The Affirmative, according to the wording of the question, are to advocate a change in our common law, while the Negative in duty bound are to oppose the proposition for change, and to defend as the Negative always defend, the order of things as they are.

The Affirmative are to advocate such a change, the abolition of the common-law defenses of the employer. For the purposes of this debate, it is immaterial to us whether this change is brought about by a simple extension of the employer's liability, or whether it is accompanied, as in many of our states, by a system of workman's compensation. Likewise, it is a consideration extraneous to the issues of this debate, whether the employer shoulder this risk himself, whether he insure it in a private insurance company, or whether he be compelled to insure it in a company managed by the state. At all events, and under any of these plans, the proposition of the Affirmative will be maintained, the employer will be deprived of his defenses at common law, and the employee will recover his damages regardless of questions of fault.

Assuming then the full burden of proof, the Affirmative propose to demonstrate that the assumption of risk and the fellow-servant rule as defined and interpreted by the common law should be abolished, first, because whatever reasons may have justified these doctrines in years gone by they have no application to industrial conditions in our day; and, secondly, because the abolition of these common law defenses will but place the burden of industrial loss, as in justice it should be placed, upon the ultimate consumer of the product of the industry.

Mr. Watson, speaking for the Negative:

The proposed abolition of these two common-law defenses, like every change of law or any suggested reform, is brought to our attention by certain existing evils. The advocates of this reform have a definite proposition in mind and that proposition is definitely and clearly stated in the question. It is a question in which people in every walk of life are concerned. Since it is of such widespread interest, let us lift it from a plane of mere debating tactics, in which a question of this kind is so often placed, and where a great deal of time is spent in arguing what the Affirmative or the Negative may stand for according to the interpretation of the question, let us lift it from that plane, and consider it as practical men and women who are interested in the outcome of this great problem. It is, then, in its larger sense, a legal question and must be considered from the standpoints of justice and of expediency.

It is not enough for the Affirmative to point out evils that exist under these two common-law rules, for there is bound to be some evil in the administration of all law; so they must further show that these evils which they have named are inherent in these two laws, and that the proposed change will remedy the existing evils. Now the Negative maintain that the evils complained of are not inherent in these laws, and we believe that the Affirmative plan is not the proper solution of the problem.

I will show you that these common-law rules are founded on principles of justice and that their removal would be unjust to the employer; second that it would discriminate against the smaller tradesmen; and third that the proposed remedy does not strike at the root of the evil, since it would affect only a small percentage of industrial accidents.

CARL SCHURZ ON GENERAL AMNESTY

(A bill being before Congress proposing to restore to leading Southerners many of the privileges which had been denied them following the war, Mr. Schurz determined the issue as follows:)

Mr. President: When this debate commenced before the holidays, I refrained from taking part in it, and from expressing my opinions on some of the provisions of the bill now before us; hoping as I did that the measure could be passed without difficulty, and that a great many of those who now labor under political disabilities would be immediately relieved. This expectation was disappointed. An amendment to the bill was adopted. It will have to go back to the House of Representatives now unless by some parliamentary means we get rid of the amendment, and there being no inducement left to waive what criticism we might feel inclined to bring forward, we may consider the whole question open.

I beg leave to say that I am in favor of general, or, as this word is considered more expressive, universal amnesty, believing, as I do, that the reasons make it desirable that the amnesty should be universal. The senator from South Carolina has already given notice that he will move to strike out the exceptions from the operation of this act of relief for which the bill provides. If he had not declared his intention to that effect, I would do so. In any event, whenever he offers his amendment I shall most heartily support it.

In the course of this debate we have listened to some senators, as they conjured up before our eyes once more all the horrors of the Rebellion, the wickedness of its conception, how terrible its incidents were, and how harrowing its consequences. Sir, I admit it all; I will not combat the correctness of the picture; and yet if I differ with the gentlemen who drew it, it is because, had the conception of the Rebellion been still more wicked, had its incidents been still more terrible, its consequences still more harrowing, I could not permit myself to forget that in dealing with the question now before us we have to deal not alone with the past, but with the present and future of this republic.

What do we want to accomplish as good citizens and patriots? Do we mean only to inflict upon the late rebels pain, degradation, mortification, annoyance, for its own sake; to torture their feelings without any ulterior purpose? Certainly such a purpose could not by any possibility animate high-minded men. I presume, therefore, that those who still favor the continuance of some of the disabilities imposed by the Fourteenth Amendment do so because they have some higher object of public usefulness in view, an object of public usefulness sufficient to justify, in their minds at least, the denial of rights to others which we ourselves enjoy.

What can those objects of public usefulness be? Let me assume that, if we differ as to the means to be employed, we are agreed as to the supreme end and aim to be reached. That end and aim of our endeavors can be no other than to secure to all the States the blessings of good and free government and the highest degree of prosperity and well-being they can attain, and to revive in all citizens of this republic that love for the Union and its institutions, and that inspiring consciousness of a common nationality, which, after all, must bind all Americans together.

What are the best means for the attainment of that end? This, Sir, as I conceive it, is the only legitimate question we have to decide.

APPENDIX III

A TYPICAL COLLEGE FORENSIC

The forensic which follows is the one which was used by the State University of Iowa in its debates with the University of Wisconsin and the University of Minnesota in 1908. In the form in which it appears here it was given in a home contest a few evenings before the Inter-State Debate. It is quoted here with the permission of the Forensic League of the State University of Iowa.

Resolved, That American Cities Should Adopt a Commission Form of Government.

Mr. Clarence Coulter, the first speaker on the Affirmative, said:

It is not my purpose to picture the shame of American cities; that is well known; but I am to consider only those evils due to the present form of municipal government, an organization based on the separation of the powers into the legislative, executive, and judicial departments. The proper remedy for these evils will be secured only by adopting a form which concentrates the entire authority of city government in one definite and responsible body.

It is a significant fact, that during the last quarter of a century, the tendency in municipal organization has been toward concentration of powers. Certain of our cities have recognized the wisdom of such action, but have unwisely attempted to concentrate only the executive power whereas the real solution lies in concentrating all governmental authority in one definite and responsible body.

New York City tried such a plan and it has failed; failed because its separate legislative department has proved an obstruction to effective action. Consequently, there has been a continual tendency to deprive the council of all power, until today its only function is to vote on franchises and issue certain licenses. So evident is the imperative need of concentrating the legislative and administrative powers in one body, that there is now a charter revision committee meeting in New York whose great object is to

78

consider the advisability of entirely eliminating the separate council, and creating in its place a small commission possessing both legislative and administrative authority. Practically the same condition obtains in the city of Boston.

What is true of New York and Boston is equally true of scores of other cities. Memphis tried for years to reform her government with an isolated council. Today she is clamoring at the doors of her legislature for a commission charter. Within the past two years more than a dozen states have provided for a commission form of government, while within the past year more than a dozen cities have actually thrown away their old forms and assumed the commission system.

The success of a separate legislative body in state and national government is the only excuse for its retention in our cities, yet the failure, for over a century in all its different forms and variations, proves that such a government is unsuited to them. There are several important and fundamental characteristics of the city that demand a different form of government and show conclusively that there is no need of a separate legislative body. In the first place, the city is not a sovereign government, but is subordinate to state and nation. There is no reason for a distinct legislature to determine the broad matters of policy, for they are determined for the citizens of the city as well as those of the country, by the state and national legislatures, in which both the city and country are represented. In the second place, the work of a city is largely administrative and of a business character, as my colleagues will show, and there is no necessity for a separate council to legislate when a commissioner is better able, as we shall show, to pass the kind of legislation characteristic of the city.

In the third place, we do not find, as in the state, the necessity of a large and separate body to represent the various localities. The city has a large population living in a restricted territory; in the state it is scattered. The city is unified by means of its rapid communication and transportation facilities, and its interests are common. These, Honorable Judges, are some general reasons why there is no necessity for trying to maintain a separate legislative body at the expense of efficiency in administration and the fixing of individual responsibility.

But let us now examine as to wherein this principle of separation fails to meet modern municipal conditions. In the first place we find that this system has failed to produce efficiency, because, in actual practice, it has been impossible to keep the legislative and administrative branches within their proper spheres of action. To be sure, such difficulty does not exist in state and national governments where the work is naturally divided. But in city government, where the work is of a peculiar kind, where it is unified in character and is largely administrative and of a business nature, it has been found impossible to maintain a separation. It is not at all surprising to find that in some cities, the mayor is the dominating factor in both legislation and administration. He is the presiding officer of the council with the deciding vote, and, in addition, is clothed with the veto power. On the other hand, there are scores of instances where the council assumes administrative functions. It names all appointments to office, and it creates and controls all the departments of city government. Under such circumstances the administrative department is subordinate to the council, because its officers can be both appointed and removed by that body and because it can carry on no work without the council's authority. Thus there is an inevitable tendency to concentrate the powers in one of the two branches, yet, at the same time, diffusing responsibility between them. Such a condition only goes to show that city government is gradually but surely working its way toward concentration in one body. But the trouble lies in the fact that the present system makes possible concentration of power, without a corresponding concentration of responsibility. From such a condition have grown two grave and inherent evils. First, it has entirely eliminated the system of checks and balances, which is a fundamental doctrine of the division of power. Secondly, it has utterly destroyed all effective responsibility.

It is apparent at once, that when one branch of the government dominates, the checks and balances between the departments are immediately lost, and facts bear out what theory shows to be logically true. The system of checks and balances failed absolutely in New York, where the mayor is supreme, and where the city has been plundered of sums estimated at 7 per cent of the total valuation of real estate. It has failed in St. Louis, where the council dominated, and where "Boss Butler" paid that body $250,000 to pass a street railway franchise. Neither did it work in Philadelphia, which has been plundered of an amount equal to 10 per cent of her real estate valuation; nor in San Francisco under the disgraceful régime of Mayor Schmitz. So overwhelming is the evidence on this point that it is needless to dwell further upon it.

In the second place, this domination of one branch over the other has resulted in a lack of responsibility and of co-ordination in city affairs. These two elements are indispensable where the work to be performed is of a local and business nature. We find that under the present system, no matter which branch of government dominates, there is always a notorious lack of responsibility. If the council makes a blunder in legislation, it immediately lays the blame upon the administrative officials, maintaining that it passed the measure upon recommendation of the administrative branch, or that branch failed to carry out its policy. If the administrative officials are neglectful, they shift the blame onto the council, and insist that the difficulty lies in insufficient legislation. Under such conditions, the average citizen has no way of telling where the blame really lies.

At present, there is no attempt at co-ordination between the legislative, executive, and judicial departments. On the other hand, there is often open rupture between them. For years before the commission form of government was adopted in Galveston, there was open warfare between the legislative and executive departments, which saddled upon the city a bonded debt of many thousands of dollars. In our state, there is a municipality in which the two departments of government are defying each other. Both are exercising legislative and administrative authority until the citizens of that place are at a loss to know which is right. This is admittedly a deplorable state of affairs, yet it is the logical result of forcing upon the city a form of government entirely unsuited for its needs. Moreover, this lack of co-ordination and responsibility has resulted in the confusion of powers and the creation of needless boards and committees. A recent investigation in Philadelphia showed that it had four boards with power to tear up the streets at will, but none to see that they were properly relaid. Chicago finds herself possessed of eight different tax levying bodies, while in New York City there are eighty different boards or individuals who have power to create debt. Is it any wonder that inefficiency and graft infest such a maze of boards, councils and committees? We see, then, that the present system of separation of powers produces inefficiency through a confusion of functions; it does away completely with the system of checks and balances and results in utter lack of responsibility and co-ordination of departments.

Honorable Judges, if we are ever to arrive at a solution of our municipal problem, we must concentrate municipal authority; we must co-ordinate departments, eliminate useless boards and committees and fix absolutely and completely individual responsibility. This, we propose to do by establishing a commission form of government, where all governmental authority is vested in one small body of men, who individually act as the heads of administrative departments, but who collectively pass the needed legislation. Thus, instead of a council with restricted powers and divided authority, we have a few men assuming positions of genuine responsibility, as regards both the originating and enforcing of laws. My colleagues will show that such a concentration of powers in one small body is necessary and desirable, both from the legislative and administrative point of view.

Such a concentration is desirable, since it is accompanied by a corresponding concentration of personal responsibility. This is secured in the commission system. Responsibility in administration is secured, because each commissioner is at the head of a department, for the efficient and honest conduct of which he alone is held personally responsible. Responsibility in legislation is secured, because, first, the body of legislators is comparatively small. Second, the very fact that each commissioner possesses information essential to intelligent action, places upon the commission itself absolute responsibility. Such a system makes it impossible to shift responsibility from one branch to the other, and guarantees to us better and more efficient administration of our municipal affairs for it eliminates all useless boards and committees and fixes absolutely and completely individual responsibility.

Mr. Earl Stewart, the first speaker on the Negative, said:

We wish it understood at the outset that no one deplores the useless boards and complicated machinery in many of our American cities more than do the Negative.

Before going a step farther let us get right as to what we mean by a commission form. The gentlemen state that they are standing for a concentration of all power in one small body. Honorable Judges, they are standing for something different. It is possible to concentrate all authority in one body and yet have the different functions performed by separately constituted bodies. For example, the cabinet system of Germany, where all governing power is vested in the legislative body which in turn delegates all administrative functions to the cabinet. Thus the legislative body is directly responsible, having ultimate authority, yet the actual exercise of power is done by distinct bodies. Now how is it with the commission? There, not only does one body have ultimate authority, but it actually conducts administration as well as legislation. Quoting from Sec. 7 of the Des Moines charter, which is typical of every commission form charter in this regard, it says: "All legislative, executive, and judicial functions of the city shall be placed in the hands of the commissioners who shall exercise those functions." The Affirmative, then, are standing for fusion of functions, and not concentration of powers.

The Negative do not defend the evils of present city organization. The Negative believe that far-reaching reforms must be instituted before we shall enjoy municipal success. The issue then is, does the commission form, or do the reforms proposed by the Negative, offer the more satisfactory solution of our municipal problems?

The Negative propose, first, that the form of organization shall embody a proper correlation or departments.

In the early council system the functions of the legislative and executive departments so overlapped that there was continual conflict of authority. Under the board system the two departments were almost disconnected, so that the legislative department could not hold the executive accountable to the will of the people. In many forms today, as the gentlemen have depicted, the relations between the departments are such that responsibility cannot be fixed.

But, Honorable Judges, these instances of failure do not show that it is impossible to preserve a proper division of functions, for every conspicuous example of municipal success in the world is based upon the proper correlation between the legislative and administrative departments. Municipal success in Europe is an established fact. There we find the cabinet form. A similar form is in vogue in Toronto, Canada, which Mayor Coatswain says is most gratifying to the public. Says Rear Admiral Chadwick: "The city of Newport, Rhode Island, has now a form of government that awakens the interest of the citizens, keeps that interest awake, and conducts its affairs in obedience to the wishes of the majority." Charleston, S. C., Elmira, New York, Los Angeles, Cal., are but a few of the typical American cities which have successfully adopted the ordinary mayor and council form. Says Mayor Rhett, of Charleston: "I am the executive of a city that has been under a mayor and council for over one hundred years. It is quite as capable of prompt action on any matter as any business corporation." The National Municipal League, composed of such men as Albert Shaw, of New York City, and Professor Rowe of the University of Pennsylvania, appointed a committee to formulate a definite program of reform. This committee did not even consider the abandoning of distinct legislative and administrative bodies, but, after three years of unremitting effort, presented a working system, embodying, in the words of the committee itself, the "essential principle of all successful government," namely, the proper correlation between the legislative and administrative departments. That program has left marked traces in the constitution of Virginia, Alabama, Colorado, New York, Wisconsin, Michigan, and Delaware.

Proper correlation between departments is best facilitated in the cabinet form, because all governing power is vested in the legislative body, which in turn delegates all administrative functions to the cabinet. However, many cities have properly correlated mayor and council by utilizing the model charter of the National Municipal League. The Negative, therefore, is here to promulgate no specific form for all American cities: conditions in Boston may require a different mechanism from that in San Francisco, but whatever form, the underlying principle of a proper division of functions must be embodied. The Affirmative must admit that proper correlation of departments has brought about municipal success, as far as mere organization can do so, yet, notwithstanding that, after fifteen years of misrule under the commission form in Sacramento the freeholders by unanimous choice again adopted distinct legislative and administrative bodies; and that the commission form has lately operated but a few years in a few small cities, amid aroused civic interest. The Affirmative would abolish at one blow the working principle of successful city organization in France, Germany, England, Canada, and unnumbered cities in the United States.

In the second place, evils in our cities are due to bad social and economic conditions. Harrisburg, Pa., was notoriously corrupt. A spirit of reform aroused the citizens, and Harrisburg stands today as a remarkable example of efficient government, yet the form of organization has been unchanged.

In many of our large cities there is a feeble civic spirit, due, in part, to undesirable immigrants, the prey to the boss, and utterly lacking in inherited traditions so essential to the capacity of self-government. Another instance: the mutual taxing system has fostered public extravagance and loss of interest on the part of the taxpayer. Again, favor-seeking corporations have continually employed corrupt methods. James Bryce says that in the development of a stronger sense of civic duty rather than any change in the form of government lies the ultimate hope of municipal reform.

A third cause of municipal ills is that of poor business methods. First, unjust election laws and lack of proper primaries have permitted the corrupt arts of the caucus politician. Second, lack of a uniform system of accounting has served only to conceal the facts, resulting in apathy on the part of the people, diffusion of responsibility, and widespread corruption among officials. Third, lack of publicity of proceedings has protected graft. Fourth, lack of civil service has perpetuated the spoils system.

All these can and are being remedied. The Bureau of Municipal Research shows plainly that it is not necessary to change fundamental principles to secure business efficiency. It reorganized the Real Estate Bureau of New York that eluded all graft charges and made 100 per cent profits. The Department of Finance, heretofore unable to tell whether taxes were collected, is reorganized from top to bottom. Through the glaring light of publicity, the bureau collected more than a million dollars for paving done at the public's expense between the street-car company's rails. The old conditions, where examination of the books of any department involved weeks of labor, have given way to a uniform system of public accounting. In the words of the Springfield, Mass., *Republican*, "The work of the Bureau of Public Research is far more fundamental than the question of substituting city organization with a commission."

A fourth cause of evils is that of state interference in purely local affairs.

In the United States the city may not act except where authorized expressly and especially by the state. In Europe the city may do anything it is not forbidden to do, and municipal success there is based on this greater freedom. The European city, though subject to general state law, makes its own local laws, not in conflict with, but in addition to, state law. But in the United States the state legislature, accustomed to interfere in matters of interest to the state government, failed to distinguish between such matters and those of exclusive interest to the cities themselves. To illustrate: The Cleveland Municipal Association reported in 1900 that legislators from an outside county had introduced radical changes in almost every department of their city government. In Massachusetts the police, water works, and park systems are directly under the state, and the only part the cities have is to pay the bills. In Pennsylvania for thirty-one years the state kept upon the statute books an act imposing upon Philadelphia a self-perpetuating commission, appointed without reference to the city's wishes, and with all power to erect a city hall and levy taxes to collect the twenty-million-dollar cost.

State and national political parties, controlling the legislature, have meddled in the private affairs of the city, resulting in the decay of the city council and the destruction of the local autonomy. Professor Goodnow says that under these conditions a scientific solution of the vexed question of municipal organization has been impossible.

The remedy lies in restoring to the city its proper field of legislation. Already thirty states have passed constitutional amendments granting greater legislative powers to the cities. Five states now allow cities to amend their own charters. But in direct opposition to this movement for municipal home rule, the commission form takes the last step in the destruction of the city's legislative body and fosters continued state interference. President Eliot says that the functions of the commissioners will be defined and enumerated by the state.

Now, Honorable Judges, the basic principle of city government the world over is division of functions. It is the principle that the commission form attempts to annihilate. But we have pointed out the real causes of municipal evils and have shown they are to be remedied without tampering with the fundamental principles which time and experience have shown to be correct in every instance of successful city organization. The Affirmative say: change the fundamental principle; all changes in form and other remedies are insufficient. The Negative say: retain the principle of distinct legislative and administrative bodies, but observe a proper correlation between them which is done in countless instances as we have shown. We would remedy bad social and economic conditions, introduce better business methods, and, most important of all, give the city greater freedom in powers of local self-government.

Mr. Clyde Robbins, the second speaker of the Affirmative, said:

It should be understood at the outset that the Affirmative desire all the local self-government for American cities that the Negative can induce the state legislatures to give them. But just what is home rule for cities? It is simply granting additional functions to the city by the state legislature. The only possible way home rule can affect the question under discussion is a consideration of which form of government is best suited to perform additional functions granted by the government. We maintain that the commission form can do this better because, first, it furnishes superior legislation, and second, it furnishes superior administration.

The gentleman blandly assumes that the commission form is fundamentally wrong, because it fails to provide a separate legislative body as do the governments of the state and nation. An isolated legislative body is desirable for state and national governments. Is that a reason for applying it to city government? Here, social, economic, and political conditions are entirely different from those of either state or nation. The city is not a sovereign body. Its powers are exclusively those delegated to it by the state legislature. They are confined wholly to matters of local concern. Furthermore, we do not deny the legislative functions of the city, nor does the plan we advocate contemplate the destruction of the city's legislative body. It simply means that in place of the present notoriously inefficient, isolated council, we establish a commission council composed of the heads of the various administrative departments. The question at issue is not whether we shall have a city council, either system provides for that; but whether a commission council, or an isolated council will furnish better ordinances. We are contending that the commission council must furnish superior measures, because in the making of city ordinances there are at least three great essentials for which this commission council alone makes adequate provision.

First the legislative and administrative work of the city must be unalterably connected;

Second, the councilmen must have a direct and technical knowledge of the city affairs;

Third, the councilman must be representative of the whole city.

Consider, first, how the legislative and administrative work are connected. State and national legislation are general in their nature and scope. The extent of territory, and the variety in local needs have naturally created a separate law-making body. But in the city such conditions do not exist. The legislative acts of the council are specific in their nature. The very name reveals their distinctive character. They are ordinances as distinguished from other laws, and are designed to meet a particular kind of administration. The specific act and the particular administration of it go hand in hand. Hence, satisfactory measures can be enacted only when they come from the hands of a commission council.

President Eliot recognized this fact when he said that the work of the city council is not concerned with far-reaching policies of legislation. There is no occasion for two or even one separate legislative body. Dr. Albert Shaw writes, that so indistinguishably blended are the legislative and administrative departments of the city, that it is impossible to separate one from the other.

Second, a commission council is more effective because it furnishes a direct and technical knowledge of city affairs. An investigation in Des Moines showed that out of 370 acts performed by the council, 32 were granting of saloon licenses and similar permits; 338 concerned matters demanding technical knowledge. To have a street paved, shall one body legislate; a second group administer; and a third pass upon the validity of the whole thing? Rather the councilmen should know good paving; they should know how to draw up and enforce a business contract. These are the vital necessities.

The commission council secures such results. Its membership is comparatively small. Its sessions are held daily. Its members have a direct knowledge of the city's needs for each one serves as the head of a department. Satisfactory legislation then becomes a mere business proposition. It is but carrying forward the work of each commissioner, for successful administration is impossible without competent legislation. Hence, a city commissioner would no more think of passing improper legislation than a bank director would think of advising unsound loans.

The Cedar Rapids commission met to legislate on replacing an old bridge. The commissioner of public safety told in what respects the old structure was unsafe. The commissioner of public property knew how much land the city owned abutting the bridge. The commissioner of streets explained what alterations should be made in the approaches, and the commissioner of finance knew in just what way the city could best pay for the improvement. Honorable Judges, such men are in a position to legislate with thoroughness. They are a commission council, the very nature of which makes it inevitable that they act with intelligence and efficiency.

Contrast now, the commission council with the isolated council. Here we find positively no co-ordination between the legislative and administrative branches, while a century of experience with the scheme of checks and balances has proved conclusively that it can not prevent municipal corruption. Moreover, legislation by the isolated council is not only chaotic in form but it is irresponsible, while in the case of the commission council the very fact that the head of each department possesses necessary information not only secures adequate legislation but fixes with certainty the entire responsibility.

The isolated council is a large and unwieldy body. Each member of it has his own private occupation. Without special preparation of any kind he attends council not oftener than once a week. Intelligent action under such conditions is simply impossible. The only way this council has of securing reliable information is from the heads of the administrative departments. But even then responsibility is still divided between the legislative and administrative branches. This deplorable state of affairs has been synchronous with the growth of the isolated council in America.

Is it any wonder that the old Des Moines council voted to construct a bridge only to find when the work was completed that the city did not even own the approaches, or that the old Cedar Rapids council let a similar contract at an exorbitantly high price, only to find, when the work was completed, that the contract called for no protecting wings or abutments, and the city was compelled to spend many thousands of dollars additional in order to make the structure safe? Such nonsensical legislation is a direct result of the isolated council. It fails to provide nformation essential to intelligent action. It does not permit a proper co-ordination of departments so vitally necessary in successful city government.

Lastly, city legislation demands unbiased representation. In this respect a commission council is superior to an isolated council.

In the commission council each member represents the entire city. Hence, there is no incentive to favor one ward at the expense of another. In fact, any such an attempt could result only in disaster to the commissioner himself. Furthermore, each commissioner is held individually responsible for his department. Consequently he is forced to insist upon an impartial representation of the entire city. This is well illustrated by the present situation in New York City. The Bureau of Municipal Research, admittedly the most practical organization of its kind in the country, is conducting its work along the line of effective competency in city departments. As a result of its investigations, the citizens of New York have been forced to the conclusion to which my colleague has already referred, namely, that the ultimate solution of their municipal difficulties will be reached only when they have disposed of their present inefficient and useless ward council and created in its place a commission council.

Under the isolated council a member is elected to represent a certain section of the city. He must do this, no matter what may be the effect upon the rest of the city. For example, in legislating on the annual budget, each ward boss brings pressure to bear upon his own councilman to have certain levies reduced, and to secure stipulated appropriations for his own ward. In New York City last spring, Bird S. Coler, representing a part of Brooklyn, blocked every appropriation until he secured certain selfish measures for his own district. What is true of New York is an annual occurrence in practically every other ward-ruled American city.

Furthermore, councilmen from one ward are shamefully unresponsive to the needs and desires of citizens in other wards. Just this summer the council of Duluth, Minn., granted saloon licenses for a ward in which 90 per cent of its citizens signed a written protest against such action. The councilmen representing that district were helpless to prevent the legislation and the citizens themselves had no recourse whatsoever. The grand jury in St. Louis reported that the wards of that city were an actual menace to decency and good government.

With these instances before us it is well to remember that the scheme of ward representation is a necessary part of the practical operation of the separation of powers in government. This is exemplified in our national, state, and city organizations. In fact, the principal reason for an isolated legislative body is that the sentiments of the different localities may be expressed in legislation. The practical result is that 95 per cent of our city governments are based upon ward representation, nor can an instance be cited in all American political theory which shows the creation of a successful political organization based upon an isolated legislative body in which there has not been an accompanying representation by territorial districts. This principle is always the same no matter whether it be a congressional district of the national government or a ward of the city government. Hence, it is for this principle that the gentlemen must contend if they wish to argue for an isolated council in city government.

In conclusion, Honorable Judges, a commission council is superior to an isolated council, because the work of city legislation and administration must be unalterably connected; because the councilmen must have a direct and technical knowledge of city affairs; and, because the councilmen must be representative of the whole city.

Mr. Vincent Starzinger, the second speaker on the Negative, said:

The Affirmative continue to direct their attack against the "old form." Yet my colleague has suggested substantial changes in present city organization, changes which have brought about success wherever tried. Moreover, we wish to make it clear that we are not necessarily standing for a division of power. There may be separately constituted departments of government, one primarily for administration, the other primarily for legislation, yet a concentration of authority in one of them, as in the case under the cabinet system of Europe. The gentlemen of the opposition are advocating not only a concentration of power, but a fusion of functions as well. Their commission is at once the executive cabinet and the legislative body.

We have heard much about the practical working of the new plan. Upon this matter, the Negative shall have a few words to say before the close of the debate. But granting for the sake of argument that the commission form has operated with some degree of success in a few small towns, especially when compared with the admitted inefficient machinery of government in vogue before its adoption and when favored by an aroused civic interest, nevertheless, it does not follow that it is adapted to the needs of the typical American city. There, administration is a matter of great complexity and of vital importance. Boston has pay-rolls including 12,000 and annual expenditure of $40,000,000. Suc-'cessful administration under such conditions has necessitated the growth of city departments. The heads of the various departments constitute an executive cabinet. Under the commission form, this cabinet is established by popular election and made the single governmental body for the performance of both the legislative and the administrative functions.

Such a fusion of functions must necessarily result: in poor administration; in the sacrifice of legislation; and in the ultimate destruction of local self-government.

Consider the problem of administration.

An efficient cabinet cannot, as a rule, be secured by popular election. Men who possess the ability to direct a city department acquire such capacity only after years of preparation, and such men will not endure the uncertainties of a career dependent upon the favor of the public. The commissioner of finance who understands the intricate problems of accounting will not coddle the people to insure his election. Popular judgment, no matter how enlightened, cannot be entrusted with the selection of such men. The old board system proves this conclusively. Here, the choosing of the heads of the important city departments was placed in the hands of the people. The system stands condemned.

A commission form makes the additional blunder of uniting completely the two functions of legislation and administration in the same body. This makes the commissioners representative in character. But this condition is disastrous to successful administration. Whenever the people desire even the slightest change in their local policy, the stability and continuity of the city departments must be upset. Representation is secured at the expense of efficiency. Administration becomes saturated with politics.

Again, Honorable Judges, the management of a city should be subjected to the criticism and control of a reviewing body. Both the welfare of the people and the interests of good administration demand it. Administrators, no matter how valuable their technical knowledge, make poor legislators. Being interested in their work, they very naturally exalt and magnify their departments. Just a few years ago, the city of Cleveland found it necessary to take even the preparation of the budget from the heads of the departments concerned and to place it with a board which could view with impartiality the demands of the various department chiefs. Think of turning over all the functions of a city like St. Louis to an executive cabinet without even the oversight or criticism of an impartial body.

And, Honorable Judges, the whole experience of government proves the absolute necessity for a separate legislative department. Look where you will, and in each case there is an executive cabinet, based upon appointment, untrammelled by the burdens of legislation, and subjected to the criticism and control of a reviewing body. In Europe, the city councils are elected by the people, and the administrative departments are made up through a process of selection and appointment, together with the assurance of reasonable permanence of tenure, responsibility, and adequate support. Likewise in America, the larger cities are already organizing their cabinets upon a somewhat similar basis. The six largest cities of New York, all of the cities of Indiana, Boston, Chicago, Baltimore, and many others are securing their important administrative officials through appointment by the mayor. This is the general plan advocated by the National Municipal League. It centers responsibility for the administration in one man.   On the other hand, some of the cities of Canada follow more closely to the German system.   There the cabinet is selected by a representative council.   In practically all of these instances, men of special ability have been obtained, the departments of administration have been properly correlated, responsibility has been concentrated, and the general principle, that successful administration depends upon a separately constituted legislative body, has been firmly established.

It is plain then that a commission form violates the fundamental principles of successful administration.   It first attempts to secure a cabinet by popular vote.   It then upsets the stability of the city departments by completely uniting both the legislative and the administrative functions.   Finally, it destroys the responsibility of that prime essential of successful administration, namely, a proper reviewing body.

In the second place, Honorable Judges, the permanent adoption of a commission form must necessarily mean a sacrifice of legislation and the ultimate destruction of local self-government.   Even though the city may be subordinate to the state, nevertheless, it has a broad field of independent action.   Otherwise, why give it a separate personality and a separate organization?   Cities are permitted to exercise vast powers of police and of taxation. It is idle to say that a few commissioners can give satisfactory legislation.   They cannot represent community interests.   Their executive functions will naturally bias their judgment.   Moreover, each commissioner, knowing little of the needs of the other departments, will naturally take the word of its administrative head, especially since he desires the same freedom.   This was actually the case in Sacramento, Cal., where the commission plan was tried for fifteen years and given up as an abject failure. Says the Hon. Clinton White of that city: "In almost every instance, the board soon came to the understanding that each man was to be let alone in the management of the department assigned to him.   This resulted in there being in fact no tribunals exercising a supervisory power over the executive of a particular department."   Honorable Judges, a reviewing and legislative body is indispensable in city government and a commission makes no such provision.   Weak in administration, wholly lacking in matters of legislation, dangerous as a theory of government, it cannot help but result in the complete subjection of local government to the state. The inevitable result of its permanent adoption will be that the important local legislative functions will become a mere administrative board with discretionary power as in the case of Washington, D.C. In the words of Professor Goodnow: "The destruction of the city council has not destroyed council government. It has simply made local policy a matter of state legislative determination." If we wish to destroy the life of the city, make it impotent to discharge the functions for which it was organized, then, and then only, it might be feasible to place over it a commission.

But, Honorable Judges, authorities are agreed that cities must be allowed greater freedom of action in local affairs, that municipal home rule is indispensable. The governments of our large cities have been dominated to such an extent by the state legislatures, usually partisan and irresponsible to the locality concerned, that in many cases self-government has become a term, hollow and without meaning.

The gentlemen condemn the city council, yet they pass over the real cause for its decay. Restore to the city its proper legislative powers, confine the work of the council to legislation instead of allowing it to go into details of administration, reduce the number of councilmen, if necessary, adjust the method of representation, introduce needed electoral and primary reform, establish responsibility by means of uniform municipal accounting and publicity of proceedings, and we ask the gentlemen in all earnestness why American city councils will not take on new life just as the city councils of every other country have done in the past.

The two great problems of American city government are: first, administration; secondly, municipal home rule. The solution of both depends upon the existence of two separately constituted departments of government. This principle is being emphasized by the leading scholars of political science, as illustrated by the program of the National Municipal League. In fact, Honorable Judges, every deep-seated reform in our large cities for the past quarter of a century has tended toward this cardinal doctrine of municipal success. The Ohio Municipal Code Commission, after two years of careful study and observation, presented a bill based upon the principles which we defend tonight, namely, a separation of administration from legislation, and secondly, municipal home rule.

In direct opposition to this, the gentlemen present and advocate as a permanent scheme for the organization of American
cities, both large and small, a commission form, a quasi-legislative
and administrative board patterned to give mediocrity in the
performance of both functions, success in neither; a form which
destroys forever the possibility of developing an efficient executive
cabinet and is entirely out of harmony with the advancing idea
of municipal home rule.

Mr. George Luxford, the third speaker on the Affirmative,
said:

It has been made very clear by my colleagues that the present
shameful condition of many of our American cities is due in large
measure to the peculiar form of the government patterned after
a scheme which is adapted to a sovereign government like the
state or nation. The Negative demand an isolation which history
shows, so far as our American cities are concerned, leads to a
complete confusion of functions, with a consequent loss of responsibility. Knowing the inadequacy of the scheme they then
demanded municipal home rule; but we have shown that the
Affirmative are thoroughly committed to municipal home rule
which under the commission form alone can be safely intrusted
to cities. State interference in city government is the child of the
form of government for which our friends of the Negative are
sponsors. Thus far the gentlemen have failed to disprove the
points which we have presented that the theory of checks and
balances when applied to American cities has failed; that the
plan of concentrating municipal authority under one head as
advocated by the commission plan is in complete harmony with
modern industrial and social development, and that the plan is
superior from a legislative standpoint. It shall be my purpose
to show that it is superior from the standpoint of administration.
We believe this because the commission lends itself to the application of business methods. The plan provides for a comparatively small body of men who meet in daily session and who give
their whole time to the work of governing the city. At present,
too often the real business of the officials is anything else. They
give their spare time to the city and we have seen the results.
Honorable judges, we claim that there is a special virtue in the
very smallness of the number inasmuch as they are properly

paid, devote all their time to their work, and are made in fact governors of the city. They have a great deal of work to do and they do it, while under our present systems the councilmen have comparatively little to do and they fail to do that little efficiently.

The reason why this small body can administer with dispatch and efficiency is seen at a glance. Each commissioner is the head of a department for which he is personally responsible. He is not hindered as is the executive at present by an inefficient and meddling council which has more power, often, than the executive himself. He knows the laws for he has helped to make them. It is his business to see that they are executed, and if they are not, he cannot escape blame. He cannot plead ignorance, lack of responsibility, or lack of power as do present administrative officers.

Moreover, this body is admirably constituted for effective carrying out of city business. It is larger than the single headed executive and possesses, therefore, a division of work which makes the administration far more effective. At the same time it is smaller than the old council and for that reason is more efficient in enacting the city's peculiar kind of legislation. In actual practice, and that seems to be the real test of city government, both administration and legislation are accomplished with accuracy and dispatch. For instance, every spring for the last decade carloads of "dagoes" with their dirt and disease have come to Cedar Rapids. Every year protests have gone up to both mayor and council, but without result. Cedar Rapids has adopted a commission form of government. Last spring when the "dagoes" came the same complaints went up as usual, that because of their insanitary methods these people carried with them filth and disease. But the petitioners did not go to the city council which met once in two weeks, nor were they referred to a committee which met less often. They went directly to the commissioners who had charge of the city health and in less than twenty-four hours the "dagoes" had been notified to either clean up or leave, and they left the city. But, say the opponents of this plan, this could have been done under the old system. To be sure, but the burning fact remains that in spite of the protests of the people, it was not done.

In Houston the government was both inefficient and dishonest.

For years the annual expenditures had exceeded the income a hundred thousand dollars. The city adopted a commission form and a four hundred thousand dollar floating debt was paid off in one year out of the ordinary income of the city. At the same time the city's taxes were reduced ten per cent. In the health department alone there is a saving of from $100 to $150 per month, while a combination in the operation of the garbage crematory and pumping station saves the city $6,000 annually. These results have been accomplished under a commission plan by the application of common, everyday business principles.

Galveston adopted a commission plan, and although its taxable values were reduced twenty-five per cent by the storm of 1900, yet within six years its commissioners not only put the city on a cash basis, made improvements costing $1,000,000 annually, but actually paid off a debt of $394,000 which had been incurred by the old council, and all this was accomplished without borrowing a dollar, issuing a bond, or increasing the rate of taxation. Other cities which have adopted a commission plan are accomplishing equally as beneficial results. Hence, we maintain that the commission form of city government is superior from the standpoint of efficiency in administration.

The commission plan is superior in administration for it is adapted to the city's financial problem. The same body of men are held responsible for the levying and collecting of taxes and for the spending of the money. This is desirable because the administrative body which is to spend money knows, accurately, the city's need of revenue. They are in a position to know; it is their business. A legislative body, whether council or a board, cannot know the city's needs for money without getting the facts from the administrative body. F. R. Clow says the council does not pretend to know the city's revenue problem and they adopt the recommendation of the administrative departments. The Negative's system of division of powers simply divides the responsibility between the legislative and administrative departments for the thing which in fact has been done by the administrative department itself. Since the administrative department really dictates the budget, it should be held directly responsible for it. Therefore, we contend that the commissioners, knowing best what the budget should contain because as administrators they know the city's need for money, are the body of men pre-eminently fitted to handle the city's budget.

The commission plan is adapted to the city's financial problem because it fosters economy. Economy is the result of understanding. The commissioners knowing the city's government, not from the administrative side alone, but from the legislative side as well, are in a position to economize and in practice they have done so. The running expenses of Galveston under the commission plan have been reduced one-third. In Houston it costs $12,800 a year less to run the water and light plants than formerly, while by a combination of work in the different departments there is a saving of $9,000 annually. In Cedar Rapids, since the adoption of the commission plan, there has been a reduction in the paving contracts let of ten and one-fifth per cent, in sewerage contracts, fourteen and two-sevenths per cent, and in water contracts, twenty per cent. Immediately after the adoption of the commission plan in Des Moines the annual cost of each arc-light was reduced five dollars. Reports from all the cities using the commission plan show that by the use of business principles the commissioners have economized in the administration of the city's government.

The commission plan is adapted to the city's finances because it provides a superior safeguard. Legislative bodies in our cities have been depended upon to represent the citizens' best interest. In practice, as we have pointed out, they have not done so. Never in the history of our municipal affairs, says Henry D. F. Baldwin, has a legislative body stood out as the representatives of the people against the administrative department. Why then continue a representative body which does not in fact represent? Instead of the withered form of a council or legislative body standing between the citizen and his government the commission plan simply removes this useless obstacle and allows the citizen to participate directly in the government. This is directly in harmony with the well-established economic principle that the self-interest of the taxpayer will control where responsibility is fixed.

Mr. Charles Briggs, the third speaker on the Negative, said:

It will be well while the matter is fresh in our minds, Honorable Judges, to make a brief examination of one matter of which the Affirmative are making a feature, that the commission form affords unusual safeguards for the financial and economic interests of the city. Now, in all fairness to the scheme which is doing quite well in a very few of our smaller cities, the question ought to be raised as to what other form of city government could be devised which would provide greater opportunities for graft and corruption. A little group of autocrats is the ideal form for which the ardent corruptionists might pray. They have it in the commission form. Exemplary men in office or a constant civic interest, may prevent the commissioners from becoming a band of robbers; but are these two preventives likely always to exist? Human experience says "No." The history of New Orleans and Sacramento confirm that decision. Civic interest is bound to subside; corrupt men are sure to become commissioners. Then the oligarchy advocated by the Affirmative becomes not a "safeguard" but a band of raiders equipped by the very form of government to loot the treasury. We must insist, at this point, that our opponents have failed in their assault upon our main contention:

First, that the evils in American city government are not attributable to the fundamental principles of that government; second, that the principles underlying the proposed form are in themselves wrong and are not consonant generally with American ideals. It remains to be shown that the commission form is impracticable as a general scheme for the government of all American cities.

We can very well agree that where the commission form of government has been tried it has been productive of some good results, and further, that in certain homogeneous communities of high culture and intelligence it might work with considerable success; but that the result obtained in cities where the commission form has been tried would warrant the universal adoption of it by American cities we must deny.

We deny the wisdom of adopting the commission form for it results in inadequate responsibility; third, it could never work in the vast majority of American cities. These reasons are apparent from examinations of the commission form where it has been and is being tried, and are inherent in the plan itself.

The tremendous centralization of power under this form of city government cannot escape a critical observer. A small body of men have absolute sway over the destiny of the city. They make all laws from the minutely specified contract for a water system to all important school legislation. All franchises are engineered by them. All contracts, great and small, are let by them. The city's bonded debt is in their hands; by them the city is taxed and incumbered. Parks, police, streets, education, public buildings, engineering, finance—everything from the smallest administrative duty to the all-engrossing functions of legislation devolves upon this commission. They can vacate any office, can create any office, and without limit fix any salary they choose. The entire officialdom, outside of the commission itself, and all the employes and the servants of the city are by law made the agents, servants, and dependents of the council. The possibilities for machine power with this autocratic centralization of authority are without condition. We can demonstrate this best by giving practical illustrations taken from the active operation of the commission form. We may preface these by saying that there is nothing inherent in the commission form or any of its attributes which can insure the selection of better men for office. The members of the commission will be about the same kind of men as the ordinary city official. Minneapolis by an election at large placed in the mayor's chair its most notorious grafter. This is proved by the personnel of the commissions where the system ' is being tried. The investigating committee appointed by the city of Des Moines, quoting their exact words, say that in Houston, where the commissioners are required to stay in the city hall every day, business men do not hold those positions, although the salaries are higher than the proposed salaries of the Des Moines commissioners. One commissioner was formerly a city scavenger, another a blacksmith, justice of the peace and alderman, a third a railway conductor, fourth a dry-goods merchant, and the mayor, a retired capitalist. Mr. Pollock of Kansas City says of the Des Moines commission, "The commission as elected consists of a former police judge and justice of the peace who is mayor-commissioner at the salary of $3,500; a coal miner, deputy sheriff; the former city assessor, whose greatest success has been in public office; a union painter of undoubted honesty and integrity, but far from a $3,000 man; an ex-mayor and politician, who is perhaps the most valuable member of the new form of government, but whose record does not disclose any great business capacity aside from that displayed in public office." The Des Moines committee says of the Galveston commission: "This is a perpetual body, a potentially perfect machine. There has been no change in the membership of the Galveston commission since it was organized. The extensive power of the commissioners have enabled them to control all political factions and to completely crush the opposition. The commissioners' faction is in complete control and even goes so far as to dictate nominations for the legislature and the national congress. In Des Moines we find evidences of this machine power in the very first session of the commission. Mr. Hume was appointed chief of police because he had delivered the labor vote to Mr. Mathis. The *Daily News*, the only Des Moines paper that supported the plan, was rewarded by having three of its staff appointed to responsible positions. Mr. Lyman was appointed secretary to Commissioner Hammery, Neil Jones secretary to Mayor Mathis. Another man was appointed to an important technical position. A brakeman was appointed street commissioner because he delivered the vote of the Federation of Labor.

These are but a few of the instances where this great centralization of power has shown itself in practice to be a system permitting of unrestricted machine power and political grafting. New Orleans tried the system and abandoned it over 20 years ago because of this very reason. The inhabitants were afraid of this tremendous centralization of power.

The friends of the commission idea claim for it the advantage of centered responsibility; but practice has proved that this form of city government is actually formulated to defeat responsibility. By the construction of this governing body each commissioner is held responsible for his respective department. But regulation for each department is made not by the commission as a whole but by the whole commission. This results in a confusion of powers. Thus in the city of Des Moines, Mr. Hume, the personal enemy of Commissioner Hammery was made chief of police by three other members of the commission for political reasons.

Who is responsible for the mistakes of Mr. Hume? The people say Hammery. But Hammery says: "I had nothing to do with his appointment." It has actually happened time and again at the commission table in Des Moines that regulations for the financial department were made by the police commission, the street commissioner and the commissioner of parks and public buildings; that the police commissioner would have the deciding vote on some important school legislation; or the commissioner of education control the appointment of policemen. This defect has given rise to log-rolling. Bridges have been built as a personal favor to one commissioner whose vote is needed to construct a new schoolhouse. Large paving and building contracts are let simply because the police commissioner wanted to oust some unfaithful political dependent. In this way each commissioner gains great favor with the voters and at the same time can escape personal responsibility for technical mistakes by shouldering the blame onto the whole commission where his identity is lost. This department trading has found its way into the Galveston commission, claimed to have the best commission of any city under this form of government. Here we find that at the same time the prosecutor of the city cases in the police court is allowed the right to collect a fee of $10 for every criminal, drunk, or vagrant convicted, and $5 for every one who pleads guilty; a 50-year franchise is granted to the Galveston Street Railway Co. without a vote of the people, the city not to receive one cent of tax and no compensation.

So, Honorable Judges, we must consider that, while the commission form may be a temporary success in a few small cities, its permanent success there is in grave doubt. Under these conditions we do not ask that it be abolished, but that under no circumstances its application be made general in this country where other forms of city government are in practice more successful and in theory more correct.

REBUTTAL

Mr. Earl Stewart opened for the Negative:

The gentlemen contend that the work of the city is almost wholly of a business nature. Honorable Judges, if the city does not have important legislative duties, what do we mean by local self-government? The courts have held again and again that the work of the city is primarily governmental. Says Judge Dillon: "The city is essentially public and political in character." Not a business corporation in this country could place vast sums of money in the hands of four of five men without the safeguard of some supervising body. Yet New York City has an annual expenditure of $150,000,000, equaled by the aggregate of seven other American cities of 400,000 population; more than that of nations; three times that of the Argentine Republic; four times that of Sweden and Norway combined. Honorable Judges, the American people are too business-like ever to place the entire raising, appropriating, and extending of such vast sums of money, or the half, or the quarter, or the tenth of such, in the hands of five men without the adequate check and safeguard of some supervising and reviewing body, call it congress, legislature, or council.

The gentlemen condemn divisions of powers because the city's functions are of such a mixed nature and no strict line of separation can be drawn. Granted. We have emphasized repeatedly that we are not standing for division of powers; we are standing for separately constituted bodies, which shall co-operate. We are defending no system of disconnected committees which the gentlemen have spent a whole speech in attacking, and we have shown, furthermore, that the evils are only augmented by going to the other extreme and completely confusing the functions in one small body. The gentlemen see no difference between principles of government and the form or mechanism which embodies, adequately or inadequately, those principles. They forget that the National Municipal League debated for three years over detail of form, never once disagreeing as to the essential principle of distinct bodies for legislation and administration. They forget that the model charter, which is efficient because it has a proper co-ordination of departments, is based upon the same principle of separately constituted bodies as the old board system with its disconnected departments and complicated machinery. Because the machinery has been inadequate, owing to causes which the gentlemen have ignored, they would abolish the working principle which is proved correct in every instance of successful city organization, wherever found.

Just a word on this over-worked argument of centering responsibility. Accountability means that a man charged with the performance of a task shall be held undividedly responsible for it. Now the commissioners collectively legislate. They can not do this without constantly and seriously intruding upon the work of the several departments. The moment this is done, responsibility is diffused. The Hume incident, mentioned by my colleague, is abundant illustration of the way responsibility is fixed under a commission form. Says Professor F. I. Herriot, head of the department of political science in Drake University and statistician of the Iowa board of control: "A commission form cuts at the very roots of official accountability and responsibility and, strange enough, it is because its friends believe that it enhances fixing of responsibility that they propose it." This from a scholar who has watched the plan in operation. A commission form does not fix responsibility, but even granting for the sake of argument that it does, are we to sacrifice representative government for the sake of fixing responsibility? If so, then why not make it still more definite and establish one-man power? Honorable Judges, we have shown that responsibility is more effectively centered by establishing uniform accounting and publicity.

The affirmative contend that the commissioners will furnish superior legislation. Now we do not say that knowledge of administration is of no benefit in legislation. But the necessary information can be secured without confusing the functions in a small executive cabinet. In Europe it is done by making the cabinet responsible to the council. In the United States, for example, Baltimore, it is done by having the cabinet meet and co-operate with the council. Nothing can be done by withholding the information, and as a matter of fact, the city secures all the benefit of the technical training of its administrators without the disadvantage of confusion of functions.

Mr. Clarence Coulter opened for the Affirmative:

It has been argued by the Negative that the success of the commission form of government is based upon the assumption of electing good men to office, and as an illustration, that the Des Moines commissioners are inefficient members of the old city hall gang. As it happens, however, one of the commissioners is a man with a national reputation as a municipal expert, a man whose honesty and integrity have never once been questioned. The commissioner of public safety has been trained for his position by long experience in municipal affairs and is a college graduate. Admitting, however, for the sake of argument, that the gentleman's contention is true; yet the unquestioned success of the Des Moines government proves the wisdom of the commission plan, for it so centralizes individual responsibility as to require honest and efficient performance of duty on the part of each commissioner.

Now as to securing good men. In the first place, the negative did not, and cannot, cite a single city in which the commission plan has failed to secure good men. Better men are elected under the commission plan, for the number of elective offices is greatly decreased, while the responsibility and honor of the position is relatively increased. Moreover, the government is put on a business basis and the commissioners are given steady employment at a good salary. They have an opportunity to make a genuine record for themselves, as well as to serve the best interests of the city. On the other hand, the fact that responsibility is definitely centered on each commissioner will, in itself, prevent men of no ability or grafting politicians from seeking office. Political parties no longer have any opportunity of putting men of little ability into office, but instead, competent men with a genuine interest in the city affairs and with no party affiliations whatever, so far as municipal affairs are concerned, will be attracted to the position of commissioner.

The opposition go further and charge that, even though efficient men may be elected to office, the commission plan makes impossible the fixing of responsibility. They failed, however, to point out a single instance in commission-governed cities to prove their point and made no attempt to show how responsibility could be better fixed under the present system. As a matter of fact, Honorable Judges, the fixing of individual responsibility, under the present system, is utterly impossible, as we have already shown, while it is the strongest virtue of the commission plan. In matters of pure administration it is absolutely impossible for the commissioner to escape individual responsibility, for he has full charge of the administration of his own department. In matters of legislation, where the majority vote of the commission may determine a policy affecting a certain commissioner, responbility is not lost but is fixed upon those few who voted for such policy.

It has been contended that the commission form of government is unpopular and that this plan has been rejected in both Sioux City and Davenport. That these cities rejected it is true. But why? Sioux City turned it down because the constitutionality of the plan had not, at that time, been determined. Davenport refused to accept it because the grafting politicians and the political ring so dominated the city's politics that they were able to defeat the new plan and retain the old, which was best suited to the furtherance of their own ends.

The gentlemen of the opposition have argued that the present inefficiency of city government is due to the interference of the state legislatures and contend that the ultimate solution of the difficulty lies in greater municipal home rule. They are correct, Honorable Judges! The state legislature has interfered. But why? Simply because the city council has proved itself inefficient. New York City's council was in full possession of its powers when the state legislature began to interfere. Legislation by somebody was necessary. The council failed, and now the negative say, give back to the city its powers and let the council try again.

According to the gentlemen themselves, the end to be achieved is less interference of state legislatures and more home rule. It is obvious, however, that this can be accomplished only when the city itself can put forth a capable and efficient legislative body. Honorable Judges, in our second speech we proved to you, that the commission provides a small but efficient legislative body, far superior to that of an isolated council. If you want municipal home rule, establish a form of government which makes it possible.

Mr. Charles Briggs replied for the Negative:

My colleague has proved that whatever the form of government, there must be a body capable of wise legislation, in fact, that there must be a body that is primarily legislative in character no matter what its connection or relation with the other departments of government. That a small commission, burdened with administrative and judicial functions, is not a proper legislative body is at once apparent. My colleague has demonstrated that this confusion of powers must result in inefficiency. But further than this, it is our contention that a body such as is the commission, without respect to the confusion of powers, without regard to the administrative duties weighing upon it, that this commission, of itself, is not suited to legislation.

There is no more reason for placing the legislation of the city of Chicago in the hands of five men than that the state legislature of Minnesota should be reduced to five members. It is true that, in many respects, the legislation of a city differs from that of a state, but it is, nevertheless, legislation, and in the larger cities particularly it is necessary that there be a representative legislative body. Five men no more constitute a proper legislative

body for 800,000 or a million people of a city than for that many
people outside the city. It is contrary to the fundamental conception of a legislative body that it be composed of a few. In no
country of free institutions is a legislative body so constituted.
My colleague has proved, and it cannot be successfully contro-
verted, that in the city, as well as in the state, there is a large field
for legislation. Why, then, should there not be a legislative body
to perform the work of legislation? Why place the work in the
hands of a body that is primarily administrative in character?

This objection alone must forever prevent the larger cities
of the United States from adopting the commission plan. Or, if
adopted, it must, for this reason alone, prove itself a failure.

Mr. Robbins replied for the Affirmative:

The Negative argue that the mechanisms of government in
Boston may differ from those of San Francisco. This is not a
discussion of the mechanisms of government. It involves deep
and fundamental principles relative to a given form of city organization. The gentlemen have not, nor cannot, cite one iota of
evidence that the underlying principles of organization in the
governments of Boston and San Francisco should be different.
The allusion to changing mechanisms is no excuse for their failure
to set in operation a definite and positive form of organization.
Yet the gentlemen have ingeniously endeavored to evade this
duty. Why have they done so? Because every system of municipal organization based upon the separation of powers—for which
the gentlemen are contending—has proved an admitted failure.

Do not the citizens of Brooklyn and San Francisco, as the citizens of every American city, like to drink pure water? Don't
they desire good transportation facilities, and aren't they glad
when they have clean streets and honest administration? Why,
then, don't the gentlemen come forward, as the Affirmative has
done, with a specific form of organization which provides for the
successful administration of the underlying features of city government? Instead, the gentlemen seem to delight in wandering
across the seas, telling what might happen if we would be indul-
gent enough to pattern our form of organization after that of
France, Germany, or Bohemia. Yet they glibly refuse to consider
that the city problem of this country is distinctly American and
is due to conditions peculiar to America.

As a matter of fact, the gentlemen have held before us the sailent features of a half dozen opposing forms of organization, none of which have succeeded individually, and the combined features of which can make nothing more than a conglomeration of theories and dogmas. Yes, the gentlemen have been painfully careful not to put their scheme into practical operation.

They talk blandly of more home rule, when it is evident that such a matter is actually beside the question at issue. In the same way they speak at length of the cabinet system of England, forgetting that the form the Affirmative is advocating involves the underlying features of the cabinet system altered to meet conditions peculiar to America. The commission form, Honorable Judges, is an evolution of the cabinet form.

Likewise they have talked much of the need for a separate reviewing body, citing the insurance scandals of New York state legislature to prove their contention. Why don't they give instances where a municipal reviewing body has checked fraud? The reason is obvious. As Henry Baldwin writes, "Never has there been an instance in American municipal history where the council has stood out against the corruption of the administrative department." Rather these so-called "reviewing bodies" are hand in hand with graft. Look at the shameful conditions of the "reviewing bodies" of Philadelphia, St. Louis, Cincinnati, and Pittsburgh, with their hands in the city treasury up to their elbows, and we realize something of the absurdity of the argument for a separate reviewing body to preserve efficiency and honesty in the city government. The people should be the reviewing body of their government. Its organization should be so simple, yet so complete, that every citizen from the educated theorist to the humblest day laborer, can review its facts with ease and understanding. This is the kind of government the commission form supplies. Why don't the gentlemen come forward with an organization equally as simple and complete?

Then the gentlemen go on to tell how they will compel the administrative officials to confer with their isolated "reviewing body," and thus secure a proper co-ordination that has failed for a century. Automatic mechanism in government can never take the place of simplicity and responsibility. Such schemes are futile. The men who can make mechanisms can break them. What we must have is a government that compels efficiency and honesty, not one which attempts to produce such results through theoretical contrivances.

Finally, the gentlemen claim that the commission form has failed in New Orleans and Sacramento. Will the gentlemen give their authority for the statement that these cities had a commission government? Every authority upon the subject which the affirmative has found points to the conclusion, that the form of government employed by these cities was not a commission form.

Mr. Starzinger closed for the Negative and said:

The Affirmative have mentioned our authority. What we have said in regard to Sacramento, Cal., is based upon excerpts from an article by the Hon. Clinton White, published in the Cedar Rapids *Evening Times*. Most of our facts concerning the southern cities which adopted the new plan are taken from the reports of the Des Moines investigation committee, headed by the Hon. W. N. Jordan. We would be glad to submit these pamphlets to the gentlemen for examination. The mere fact that Des Moines adopted the commission form does not disprove the integrity of the authorities.

It is claimed that our stand is indefinite. True, we have not offered a panacea for all municipal ills. But we have advocated numerous reforms and have pointed out countless instances of municipal success under various forms, yet all based upon the same fundamental principle, that there be separately constituted departments of government. One of the fatal objections to the gentlemen's proposition is that they are attempting to blanket the whole country with one arbitrary form, regardless of differing conditions. They have completely ignored our cases of successful city government. We demand that they explain them.

The gentlemen have said that state interference has been precipitated by the decay of the city council. Yet they advocate its complete destruction. Nothing could be more incorrect than to say that special legislation was brought on as a result of an inherent weakness in council government. Under the early council system, there was practically no state interference. About the middle of the last century, the board system was introduced and the councils were shorn of their dignity and much of their legislative power. Right there state dominion in local affairs began. These are the unbiased facts as given by Professor Goodnow in his book on city government.

In conclusion, Honorable Judges, the solution of the American city problem will be best promoted by a program of reform which strikes at the real causes of the evils, instead of the universal overturning of all traditions and theories of government in the hope of finding a short-cut road to municipal success. Give the city a proper sphere of local autonomy. Co-ordinate the departments of government, so as to establish responsibility and secure harmonious action. Simplify present city organization without destroying the two branches of government. Introduce new and improving methods, such as non-partisan primaries, civil service, uniform municipal accounting, and publicity of proceedings. Remedy bad social and economic conditions. Arouse civic interest. Do this, and there is no necessity for such a radical and revolutionary change as the universal adoption of a commission form.

The new plan means, not alone a change in the form of government, but a positive overturning of the working principle of successful city organization the world over. Its experience has been in the small towns for a short time, under unusual conditions, amid aroused public sentiment. Even here it has shown fatal weaknesses which the gentlemen have not satisfactorily explained. It was abandoned by the only large city that ever tried it; and cast aside as an abject failure by Sacramento, Cal., after fifteen years of operation. In the face of these facts, the gentlemen would have all American cities turn to this form as the final goal of municipal success; a form which attempts to revive the old board system of selecting administrative heads by popular vote; which, in addition, centers the whole government of a city in a small executive cabinet, without review or oversight; a form which, in the words of Professor Fairlie, of the University of Michigan, "is in direct opposition to the advancing idea of municipal home rule."

Mr. Luxford closed the debate for the Affirmative, and said:

The case for the Negative is now closed. It has been indefinite from start to finish. They acknowledge the success of the commission form but refuse to accept it as the proper form toward

which American cities should work. They have none to offer
except a form which is completely unknown in American cities
and successful alone in Europe under totally dissimilar conditions.
We have shown that every vital move for city improvement today
is toward a commission form, both in practice and theory. The
gentlemen have sought to overthrow the argument for the commission form, and yet suggest no possible American substitute.

But the position is not only indefinite, but it is inconsistent.
At one time they say, "the commission form is working well in
small cities." In another they declare that the commission form
ignores the only principles which are at the basis of successful
city government the world over. Putting these statements together we must conclude that the gentlemen who made the second
statement failed to hear the gentlemen who made the first. If
they grant that the commission form is successful anywhere in the
world how can it be that it is ignoring the only principles of successful city government the world over?

But we would not be unjust to the gentlemen. They are not
perhaps altogether indefinite. They would keep the old mayor
and council plan but would have non-partisan primaries, uniform
municipal accounting, and publicity of proceedings. Non-
partisan primaries and publicity of proceedings they have stolen
bodily from the commission. We are grateful to the gentlemen
for this hearty indorsement of the material features of the commission form. As to uniform municipal accounting, while it is
just as possible under the commission as under any other form
of city government, its advocacy by the gentlemen is inconsistent
with their insistent demand for municipal home rule. Who but
the state can supervise a uniform accounting of all cities? And
the gentlemen have deplored state interference.

Not only that, but the commission plan provides the necessary
responsibility whereby the citizens may know and participate
in the city government. In the first place the publication of
monthly itemized statements of all the proceedings is required.
Every ordinance appropriating money or ordering any street
improvements, or sewer, or the making of any contract shall
remain on file for public inspection at least one week before
final passage. Franchises are granted not by any legislative
body but by direct vote of the people. Similarly the citizens
retain the right to reject any ordinance passed, or to require the

passage of any needed ordinance. And finally, the citizens by direct vote may remove any commissioner at any time.

Thus we see that the commissioners know both the legislative and administrative side of the city's work, and the responsibility of doing both is fixed upon them.

Lastly, Honorable Judges, the Affirmative rest their cases upon these fundamental arguments: that the whole tendency in American city government is toward centralization of power in one body; where this concentration has been partial, city government has failed. This failure is due largely to the fact that, while power has centered, responsibility has been diffused. This unfortunate condition has been obviated by the adoption of the commission form which is found to be a success because it awakens civic interest, secures competent officials, and provides in the best possible manner for the legislative and administrative work of the city, centering power and responsibility in one small body of men.

APPENDIX IV

MATERIAL FOR BRIEFING

REPRESENTATIVE GOVERNMENT

SPEECH OF HON. CHARLES F. SCOTT, OF KANSAS, IN THE HOUSE OF REPRESENTATIVES, THURSDAY, MARCH 2, 1911

(The House having under consideration the bill [S. 7031] to codify, revise, and amend the laws relating to the judiciary.— From the *Congressional Record*, March 3, 1911.)

Mr. Speaker: In the ten years of my membership in this House I have seldom taken advantage of the latitude afforded by general debate to discuss any question not immediately before the House. But there is a question now before the country, particularly before the people of the state I have the honor to represent in part upon this floor, upon which I entertain very positive convictions, and which, I believe, is a proper subject for discussion at this time and in this place. That question, bluntly stated, is this: Is representative government a failure? We are being asked now to answer that question in the affirmative. A new school of statesmen has arisen, wiser than Washington and Hamilton and Franklin and Madison, wiser than Webster and Clay and Calhoun and Benton, wiser than Lincoln and Sumner and Stevens and Chase, wiser than Garfield and Blaine and McKinley and Taft, knowing more in their day than all the people have learned in all the days of the years since the Republic was founded.

And they tell us that representative government is a failure. They do not put this declaration into so many words—part of them because they do not know enough about the science of government to understand that the doctrines they advocate are revolutionary, and the rest of them because they lack the courage to openly declare that it is their intention to change our form of government, to subvert the system upon which our institutions are founded. But that is in effect what they propose to do.

Every school boy knows that in a pure democracy the people themselves perform directly all the functions of government, enacting laws without the intervention of a legislature, and trying causes that arise under those laws without the intervention of judge or jury; while in a republic, on the other hand, the people govern themselves, not by each citizen exercising directly all the functions of government, but by delegating that power to certain ones among them whom they choose to represent them in the legislatures, in the courts of justice, and in the various executive offices.

It follows, therefore, that to substitute the methods of a democracy for the methods of a republic touching any one of the three branches of government is to that extent to declare that representative government is a failure, is to that extent subversive and revolutionary.

Now, it does not follow by any means that because a proposed change is revolutionary it is therefore unwise. Taking it by and large, wherever the word "revolution" has come into human history it has been only another word for progress. Because a nation has pursued certain methods for a long time it does not at all follow that those methods are the best, although when a nation like the United States, so bold and alert, so little hampered by tradition, so ready to try experiments, has clung to the same methods of government for 130 years, a strong presumption has certainly been established that these methods are the best, at least for that particular nation.

But is the new system wiser than the old—in the matter of making laws, for example? The old system vests the lawmaking power in a legislative body composed of men elected by the people and supposed to be peculiarly fitted by reason of character, education, and training for the performance of that duty. These men come together and give their entire time through a period of some weeks or months to the consideration of proposed legislation, and the laws they enact go into immediate effect, and remain in force until set aside by the courts as unconstitutional or until repealed by the same authority that enacted them.

The new system—taking the Oregon law, for example, and it is commonly cited as a model—provides that 8 per cent of the voters of a state may submit a measure directly to the people, and if a majority of those voting upon it give it their support it shall become a law without reference to the legislature or to the governor. That is the initiative. And it provides that if 5 per cent of the voters are opposed to a law which the legislature has passed, upon signing the proper petition the law shall be suspended until the next general election, when the people shall be given an opportunity to pass upon it. That is the referendum.

Now, there are several things about this plan which I believe the people of this country, when they come really to consider it, will scrutinize with a good deal of care and possibly with some suspicion.

It is to be noted, in the first place, that a very few of the people can put all the people to the trouble and expense of a vote upon any measure, and the inquiry may well arise whether the cause of settled and orderly government will be promoted by vesting power in the minority thus to harass and annoy the majority. In my own state, for example, who can doubt that the prohibitory amendment, or some one of the statutes enacted for its enforcement, would have been resubmitted again and again if the initiative had been in force there these past twenty-five years.

Again, it will be observed that still fewer of the people have it in their power to suspend a law which a legislature may have passed in plain obedience to the mandate of a majority of the people, or which may be essential to the prompt and orderly conduct of public affairs, and when they come to think about it the people may wonder if the referendum might not make it possible for a small, malevolent, and mischievous minority to obstruct the machinery of government and for a time at least to nullify the will of the majority.

In the third place, it is to be remarked that a measure submitted either by the initiative or the referendum cannot be amended, but must be accepted or rejected as a whole, and we may well inquire whether this might not afford "the interests" quite as good an opportunity as they would have in a legislature to "initiate" some measure which on its face was wholesome and beneficent but within which was concealed some little "joker" that would either nullify the good features of the law or make it actively vicious, and which, through lack of discussion, would not be discovered. Every day we have new and incontestable proof that "in the multitude of counselors there is wisdom." But that wisdom can never be had under a system of legislation which lays before the people the work of one man's mind to be accepted in whole or rejected altogether.

Once more let us observe that under this system, no matter how few votes are cast upon a given measure, if there are more for it than against it, it becomes a law, so that the possibility is always present that laws may be enacted which represent the judgment or the interest of the minority rather than the majority of the people. Indeed, experience would seem to show that this is a probability rather than a possibility, for in the last Oregon election not one of the nine propositions enacted into law received as much as 50 per cent of the total vote cast, while some of them received but little more than 30 per cent of the total vote.

And finally and chiefly, without in the the least impeaching the intelligence of the people, remembering the slight and casual attention the average citizen gives to the details of public questions, we may well inquire whether the average vote cast upon these proposed measures of legislation will really represent an informed and well-considered judgment. In his thoughtful work on democracy, discussing this very question, Dr. Hyslop, of Columbia University, says:

People occupied with their private affairs, domestic and social, demanding all their resources and attention, as a rule have little time to solve the complex problems of national life. The referendum is a call to perform all the duties of the profoundest statesmanship, in addition to private obligations, which are even much more than the average man can fulfil with any success or intelligence at all, and hence it can hardly produce anything better than the Athenian assembly, which terminated in anarchy. It will not secure dispatch except at the expense of civilization, nor deliberation except at the expense of intelligence. Very few questions can be safely left to its councils, and these only of the most general kind. A tribunal that can be so easily deceived as the electorate can be in common elections cannot be trusted to decide intelligently the graver and more complicated questions of public finance or private property, of administration, and of justice. It may be honest and mean well, as I believe it would be; but such an institution can not govern.

That is the conclusion reached a priori by a profound student of men and of institutions; and there is not a man who hears me or who may read what I am now saying but knows the conclusion is sound.

But, fortunately for the states which have not yet adopted the innovation, we are not obliged to rely upon academic, a priori reasoning, in order to reach a conclusion as to the wisdom of the initiative and referendum, for the step has already been taken in other states and we have their experience to guide us.

There is South Dakota, for example, where under the initiative the ballot which I hold in my hand was submitted to the people at the recent election. This ballot is 7 feet long and 14 inches wide, and it is crowded with reading matter set in non-pareil type. Upon this ballot there are submitted for the consideration of the people six legislative propositions. Four of them are short and comparatively simple. But here is one referring to the people a law which has been passed at the preceding session of the legislature dividing the state into congressional districts. How many of the voters of South Dakota do you suppose got down their maps and their census reports and carefully worked out the details of that law to satisfy themselves whether or not it provided for a fair and honest districting of the state? They could not amend it, remember, they had to take it as it was or vote it down. In point of fact, they voted it down; but who will say that in doing this they expressed an enlightened judgment or merely followed the natural conservative instinct to vote "no" on a proposition they did not understand? And here is a law to provide for the organization, maintenance, equipment, and regulation of the National Guard of the state. This bill contains 76 sections. It occupies 4 feet 4 inches of this 7-foot ballot. It would fill two pages of an ordinary newspaper.

And here is a copy of the Oregon ballot, from which it appears that the stricken people of that commonwealth were called upon at the late election to consider 32 legislative propositions. Small wonder that it was well onto a month after election before the returns were all in.

And here is another constitutional amendment in which the people are asked to pass judgment on such simple propositions as providing for verdict by three-fourths of jury in civil cases, authorizing grand juries to be summoned separately from the trial jury, permitting change of judicial system by statute prohibiting retrial where there is any evidence to support the verdict, providing for affirmance of judgment on appeal notwithstanding error committed in lower court and directing the Supreme Court to enter such judgment as should have been entered in the lower court, fixing terms of Supreme Court, providing that judges of all courts be elected for six years, subject to recall, and increasing the jurisdiction of the Supreme Court. Is it any wonder that with questions such as those thrust at them so large a percentage of the voters took to the "continuous woods where rolls the Oregon" and refused to express a judgment one way or the other? Now, with all possible deference to the intelligence and the diligence of the good people of Oregon, is it conceivable that any considerable proportion of the voters of that commonwealth went to the polls with even a cursory knowledge of all the measures submitted for their determination?

As to the practical working of the referendum, I have seen it stated in the public prints that four years ago nearly every appropriation bill passed by the Oregon legislature was referred to the people for their approval or rejection before it could go into effect. As a result, the appropriations being unavailable until the election could be held, the state was compelled to stamp its warrants "not paid for want of funds," and to pay interest thereon, although the money was in the treasury. The university and other state institutions were hampered and embarrassed, and the whole machinery of government was in large measure paralyzed. In other words, under the Oregon law a pitiful minority of the people was able to obstruct and embarrass the usual and orderly processes of government, and for a time at least to absolutely thwart the will of an overwhelming majority of the people.

A system of government under which such a thing as that is not only possible, but has actually occurred, may be "the best system ever devised by the wit of man," as we have been vociferously assured, but some of us may take the liberty of doubting it.

But the initiative and referendum, subversive as they are of the representative principle, do not compare in importance or in possible power for evil with the recall. The statutes of every state in this Union provide a way by which a recreant official may be ousted from his office or otherwise punished. That way is by process of law, where charges must be specific, the testimony clear, and the judgment impartial. But what are we to think of a procedure under which an official is to be tried, not in a court by a jury of his peers and upon the testimony of witnesses sworn to tell the truth, but in the newspapers, on the street corners, and at political meetings? Can you conceive of a wider departure from the fundamental principles of justice that are written not only into the constitution of every civilized nation on the face of the earth, but upon the heart of every normal human being, the principle that every man accused of a crime has a right to confront his accusers, to examine them under oath, to rebut their evidence, and to have the judgment finally of men sworn to render a just and lawful verdict.

Small wonder that the argument oftenest heard in support of a proposition so abhorrent to the most primitive instincts of justice is that it will be seldom invoked and therefore cannot do very much harm. I leave you to characterize as it deserves a law whose chief merit must lie in the rarity of its enforcement.

But will it do no harm, even if seldom enforced? It is urged that its presence on the statute books and the knowledge that it can be invoked will frighten public officials into good behavior. Passing by the very obvious suggestion that an official who needs to be scared into proper conduct ought never to have been elected in the first place, we may well inquire whether the real effect would not be to frighten men into demagogy—and thus to work immeasurably greater harm to the common weal than would ever be inflicted through the transgressions of deliberately bad men.

We have demagogues enough now, heaven knows, when election to an office assures the tenure of it for two or four or six years. But if that tenure were only from hour to hour, if it were held at the whim of a powerful and unscrupulous newspaper, for example, or if it could be put in jeopardy by an affront which in the line of duty ought, we will say, to be given to some organization or faction or cabal, what could we expect? Is it not inevitable that such a system would drive out of our public life the men of real character and courage and leave us only cowards and trimmers and time servers? May we not well hesitate to introduce into our political system a device which, had it been in vogue in the past, would have made it possible for the Tories to have recalled Washington, the copperheads to have recalled Lincoln, and the jingoes to have recalled McKinley?

In all the literature of the age-long struggle for freedom and justice there is no phrase that occurs oftener than "the independence of the judiciary." Not one man could be found now among all our ninety millions to declare that our Constitution should be changed so as to permit the President in the White House or the Congress in the Capitol to dictate to our judges what their decisions should be. And yet it is seriously proposed that this power of dictation shall be given to the crowd on the street. That is what the recall means if applied to the judiciary; and it means the destruction of its independence as completely as if in set terms it were made subject to the President or the Congress.

Do you answer, "Oh, the recall will never be invoked except in an extreme case of obvious and flagrant injustice"? I reply, "How do you know? It is the theory of the initiative that it will never be invoked except to pass a good law, and of the referendum that it will never be resorted to except to defeat a bad law; but we have already seen how easily a bad law might be initiated and a good law referred. And so it is the theory that the recall will be invoked only for the protection of the people from a bad judge. What guaranty can you give that it will not be called into being to harrass and intimidate a good judge? There never yet was a two-edged sword that would not cut both ways.

Mr. Chairman, I should be the last to assert that our present system of government has always brought ideally perfect results. Now and then the people have made mistakes in the selection of their representatives. Corrupt men have been put into places of trust, small men have been sent where large men were needed, ignorant men have been charged with duties which only men of learning could fitly perform. But does it follow that because the people make mistakes in so simple a matter as the selection of their agents, they would be infallible in the incomparably more complex and difficult task of the enactment and interpretation of laws? There was never a more glaring non sequitur, and yet it is the very cornerstone upon which rests the whole structure of the new philosophy. "The people cannot be trusted with few things," runs this singular logic, "therefore let us put all things into their hands."

With one breath we are asked to renounce the old system because the people make mistakes, and with the next breath we are solemnly assured that if we adopt the new system the people will not make mistakes. I confess I am not mentally alert enough to follow that sort of logic. It is too much like the road which was so crooked that the traveler who entered upon it had only proceeded a few steps when he met himself coming back. You cannot change the nature of men, Mr. Chairman, by changing their system of government. The limitations of human judgment and knowledge and conscience which render perfection in representative government unattainable will still abide even after that form of government is swept away, and the ideal will still be far distant.

Let it not be said or imagined, Mr. Speaker, that because I protest against converting this Republic into a democracy therefore I lack confidence in the people. No man has greater faith, sir, than I have in the intelligence, the integrity, the patriotism, and the fundamental common sense of the average American citizen. But I am for representative rather than for direct government, because I have greater confidence in the second thought of the people than I have in their first thought. And that, in the last analysis, is the difference, and the only difference, so far as results are concerned between the new system and that which it seeks to supplant; it is the fundamental difference between a democracy and a republic. In either form of government the people have their way. The difference is that in a democracy the people have their way in the beginning, whereas in a republic the people have their way in the end—and the end is usually enough wiser than the beginning to be worth waiting for.

We count ourselves the fittest people in the world for self-government, and we probably are. But fit as we are we sometimes make mistakes. We sometimes form the most violent and erroneous opinions upon impulse, without full information or thoughtful consideration. With complete information and longer study, we swing around to the right side, but it is our second thought and not our first that brings us there. Our intentions are always right, and we usually get right in the end; but it often happens that we are not right in the beginning. It behooves us to consider long and well before we pluck out of the delicately adjusted mechanism by which we govern ourselves the checks and brakes and balance wheels which our forefathers placed there, and the wisdom of which our history attests innumerable times.

The simple and primitive life of civilization's frontier has given way to the most stupendous and complex industrial and commercial structure the world has ever known. Incredible expansion, social, political, industrial, commercial—but representative government all the way. At not one step in the long and shining pathway of the Nation's progress has representative government failed to respond to the Nation's need. Every emergency that 130 years of momentous history has developed—the terrible strain of war, the harrassing problems of peace—representative government has been equal to them all. Not once has it broken down. Not one issue has it failed to solve. And long after the shallow substitutes that are now proposed for it shall have been forgotten, representative government "will be doing business at the old stand," will be solving the problems of the future as it met the issues of the past, with courage and wisdom and justice, giving to the great Republic that government "of the people, for the people, and by the people" which is the assurance that it "shall not perish from the earth."

APPENDIX V

QUESTIONS WITH SUGGESTED ISSUES AND BRIEF BIBLIOGRAPHY

Below are several questions with issues suggested which should bring about a "head on" debate. They should be useful at the beginning of debating work or when time for preparation is somewhat limited. A brief bibliography is in each case appended.

"THE RIGHT OF SUFFRAGE SHOULD BE GRANTED TO WOMAN"

Affirmative

I. Woman wants the ballot.
II. Woman is capable of using the ballot wisely.
III. Where woman has had the ballot, the results have been beneficial to the state.

Negative

I. A majority of women do not want the ballot.
II. Woman is incapable of using the ballot wisely.
III. A benefit has not resulted in those states which have given woman the right to vote.

BRIEF BIBLIOGRAPHY

"Success of Woman's Suffrage," *Independent*, LXXIII, 334-35 (August 8, 1912).

"Suffrage Danger," *Living Age*, CCLXXIV, 330-35 (August 10, 1912).

"Teaching Violence to Women," *Century*, LXXXIV, 151-53 (May, 1912).

"Violence in Woman's Suffrage Movement: A Disapproval of the Militant Policy," *Century*, LXXXV, 148-49 (November, 1912).

"Violence and Votes," *Independent*, LXXII, 1416-19 (June 27, 1912).

"Votes for Women," *Harper's Weekly*, LVI, 6 (September 21, 1912).

"Votes for Women," *Harper's Bazaar* XLVI, 47, 148 (January, March, 1912).

"Votes for Women and Other Votes," *Survey*, XXVIII, 367–78 (June 1, 1912).

"What Is the Truth about Woman's Suffrage?" *Ladies' Home Journal*, XXIX, 24 (October, 1912).

"Why I Want Woman's Suffrage," *Collier's*, XLVIII, 18 (March 16, 1912).

"Why I Went into Suffrage Work," *Harper's Bazaar*, XLVI, 440 (September, 1912).

"Woman and the State," *Forum*, XLVIII, 394–408 (October 1912).

"Woman and the Suffrage," *Harper's Weekly*, LVI, 6 (August 17, 1912).

"Woman's Rights," *Outlook*, C, 262–66 (February 3, 1912).

"Woman's Rights," *Outlook*, C, 302–4 (February 10, 1912).

"Concerning Some of the Anti-Suffrage Leaders," *Good Housekeeping*, LV, 80–82 (July, 1912).

"Expansion of Equality," *Independent*, LXXIII, 1143–45 (November 14, 1912).

"Marching for Equal Suffrage," *Hearst's Magazine*, XXI, 2497–501 (June, 1912).

"Woman and the California Primaries," *Independent*, LXXII, 1316–18 (June 13, 1912).

"Woman Suffrage Victory," *Literary Digest*, XLV, 841–43 (November 23, 1912).

"Woman's Demonstration; How They Won and Used the Votes in California," *Collier's*, XLVIII, 17–18 (January 6, 1912).

"Recent Strides of Woman's Suffrage," *World's Work*, XXII, 14733–45 (August, 1911).

"Woman's Suffrage in Six States," *Independent*, LXXI, 967–20 (November 2, 1911).

"Women Did It in Colorado," *Hampton's Magazine*, XXVI, 426.

"Woman's Victory in Washington" (state), *Collier's*, XLVI, 25.

"Are Women Ready for the Franchise?" *Westminster*, CLXII, 255–61 (September, 1904).

"Argument against Woman's Suffrage," *Outlook*, LXIV, 573–74 (March 10, 1900).

"Check to Woman's Suffrage in the United States," *Nineteenth Century*, LVI, 833–41 (November, 1904).

"Female Suffrage in the United States," *Harper's Weekly*, XLIV, 949–50 (October 6, 1900).

"Ought Women to Vote?" *Outlook*, LVIII, 353–55 (June 8, 1901).

"Outlook for Woman's Suffrage," *Cosmopolitan*, XXVIII, 621–23 (April, 1900).

"Woman's Suffrage in the West," *Outlook*, LXV, 430–31 (June 23, 1900).

"Movement for Woman's Suffrage," *Outlook*, XCIII, 265–67 (October 2, 1909).

"Why?" *Everybody's*, XXI, 723–38.

"Woman's Rights," *Twentieth-Century Encyclopedia*.

"THE AMERICAN NAVY SHOULD BE ENLARGED SO AS TO COMPARE IN FIGHTING STRENGTH WITH ANY IN THE WORLD"

Affirmative

I. The scattered possessions of the United States demand the protection of a large navy.

II. The expense of the proposed navy would be a judicious investment.

III. The proposed enlargement of the navy would be a step toward universal peace.

Negative

I. The geographical situation of the United States makes a large navy unnecessary.

II. The expense entailed, if the proposed plan were put into practice, would embarrass the United States.

III. To carry out the proposed plan would be to increase the chances of war.

BRIEF BIBLIOGRAPHY

"Relative Sea Strength of the United States," *Scientific American*' CVII, 174 (August 31, 1912).

"For an Adequate Navy in the United States," *Scientific American*, CV, 512 (December 9, 1911).

"Humble Opinions of a Flat-Foot; Frank Criticism and Intimate Picture of Our Navy, by a Blue-Jacketed Gob," *Collier's* L, 14–15; P., XIX, 22–23 (December 7, 1912).

"Importance of the Command of the Sea," *Scientific American,* CV, 512 (December 9, 1911).

"The United States Fleet and Its Readiness for Service," *Scientific American,* CV, 514 (December 9, 1911).

"Battle-ship Fleet in Each Ocean," *Scientific American,* CII, 354 (April 30, 1910).

"Naval Madness," *Independent,* LXVIII, 489 (March 3, 1910).

"Our Naval Waste," *Nation,* XCI, 158 (August 25, 1910).

"Our Navy As a National Insurance," *Scientific American,* CII, 414 (May 21, 1910).

"American Naval Policy," *Forum,* XLV, 529 (May, 1911).

"If We Had to Fight," *Collier's,* XLVIII, 18 (November 18 1911).

"Panama Canal and the Sea Power in the Pacific," *Century,* LXXXII, 240 (January, 1911).

"Local Option Is the Best Method of Dealing with the Liquor Problem"

Affirmative

I. Other methods of dealing with the liquor problem have failed.

II. Local option is consistent with American ideas of government.

III. Local option is a proved success.

Negative

I. Local option is undesirable in theory.

II. Local option has not succeeded where tried.

III. There is a better method of dealing with this problem.

BRIEF BIBLIOGRAPHY

"Local Option; A Study of Massachusetts," *Atlantic,* XC, 433–40.

"Principle of Local Option," *Independent,* LIII, 3032–33 (December 19, 1901).

"When Prohibition Fails and Why," *Outlook*, CI, 639–43 (July 20, 1912).

"To Dam the Interstate Flow of Drink," *Literary Digest*, XLIV, 106–7 (January 20, 1912).

"Psychology of Drink," *American Journal of Sociology*, XVIII, 21–32 (July, 1912).

"World-Wide Fight against Alcohol," *Review of Reviews*, XLV, 374.

"Drink and the Joy of Life," *Westminster*, CLXXVI, 620–24 (December, 1911).

"Drink Traffic," *Missionary Review*, XXXII, 337–39 (May, 1909).

"Efforts to Promote Temperance since 1883," in L. B. Paton, *Recent Christian Progress*, 446–71.

"Fight against Alcohol," *Cosmopolitan*, XLIV, 492–96, 549–54 (April, May, 1908); *Harper's Weekly*, LII, 6–7 (April 25, 1908).

"Foreign Anti-Liquor Movements," *Nation*, LXXXVI, 230 (March 12, 1908).

"March of Temperance," *Arena*, XL, 325–30 (October, 1908).

"Social Conditions and the Liquor Problem," *Arena*, XXVI, 275–77 (September, 1906).

"Temperance Question," *Canadian M.*, XXXII, 282–84 (January, 1909).

"Local Option Movement," *Annals of the American Academy*, XXXII, 471–5 (November, 1908).

"Results of a Dry Year in Worcester, Mass.," *Map Survey*, XXII, 301–2 (May 29, 1909).

"Local Option and After," *North American*, CXC, 628–41 (November, 1909).

"Capital Punishment Should be Abolished"

Affirmative

I. Capital punishment does not accomplish the purpose for which it is intended.

II. Capital punishment is inconsistent with the teachings of modern criminology.

III. There are other methods of punishment far more beneficial than the death penalty.

Negative

I. Capital punishment decreases crime.

II. The cruelty of capital punishment has been greatly exaggerated.

III. Society has found no crime deterrent so powerful as the death penalty.

BRIEF BIBLIOGRAPHY

"Does Capital Punishment Prevent Convictions?" *Review of Reviews*, XL, 219-20 (August, 1909).

"Does Capital Punishment Tend to Diminish Capital Crime?" *Harper's Weekly*, L, 1028-29; *Review of Reviews*, XXXIV, 368-69 (1909).

"Meaning of Capital Punishment," *Harper's Weekly*, L, 1289 (September 8, 1906).

"Plato on Capital Punishment," *Harper's Weekly*, L, 1903 (December 29, 1906).

"Should Capital Punishment Be Abolished?" *Harper's Weekly*, LIII, 8 (July 3, 1909).

"Whitely Case and Death Penalty," *Nation*, LXXXIV, 376-77 (April 25, 1907).

"Death Penalty and Homicide," *American Journal of Sociology*, XVI, 88-116 (July, 1910); *Nation*, VIII, 166; *North American*, CXVI, 138; *ibid.*, LXII, 40; *ibid.*, CXXXIII, 534; *Forum*, III, 503; *Arena*, II, 513.

"Capital Punishment and Imprisonment for Life," *Nation*, XVI, 193.

"Capital Punishment Anecdotes from Blue Book," *Ecl. M.*, LXVI, 677.

"Capital Punishment Arguments Against," *Nation*, XVI, 213.

"Capital Punishment by Electricity," *North American*, CXLVI, 219.

"Capital Punishment: Case Against," *Fortnightly Review*, LII, 322; same article in *Eclectic Magazine*, CXIII, 518.

"The Crime of Capital Punishment," *Arena*, I, 175.

"Failure of Capital Punishment," *Arena*, XXI, 469.

"Why Have a Hangman?" *Fortnightly Review*, XL, 581.

"Punishment of Crimes," *North American*, X, 235.

APPENDIX VI

A LIST OF DEBATABLE PROPOSITIONS

Many of these, because of their local application, will be found useful for class practice where time for preparation is necessarily limited.

1. Coeducation in colleges is more desirable than segregation.

2. Textbooks should be furnished at public expense to students in public schools.

3. The adoption of the honor system in examinations would be desirable in American colleges.

4. Final examinations as a test of knowledge should be discontinued in X—— High School (or college).

5. All American universities and colleges should admit men and women on equal terms.

6. The national government should establish a university· near the center of population.

7. The X—— College (or High School) should adopt courses which more definitely fit students for practical careers.

8. Intercollegiate football does not promote the best interests of competing schools.

9. Intracollegiate athletic contests would be a desirable substitute for intercollegiate athletics.

10. Secret societies should be prohibited in public high schools.

11. National fraternities do not promote the best interests of American colleges and universities.

12. A college commons would be a desirable addition to X—— College.

13. A lunchroom should be established in the X—— High School.

14. Athletic regulations should not debar a student from playing summer baseball.

15. No student in an American college should be eligible to compete in intercollegiate athletics until he has begun his second year's work.

16. All studies in the X—— College (or High School) above those of the Freshman should be entirely elective.

17. In all public high schools training in military tactics should be required.

18. Public high schools should be under state supervision.

19. Admission to American colleges should be allowed only upon examination.

20. Academic degrees should be given only upon state examinations.

21. The library of X—— College (or High School, or city) should be open on Sunday.

22. A plan of self-government should be adopted for the X—— College (or High School).

23. The terms "successful" and "failed" as the only indication of grade work should be adopted by the X—— School in place of the present plan or working.

24. Gymnasium work should be required in X—— School.

25. Training in domestic science should be required o all girls at X—— School.

26. Manual training should be a requirement of all boys at X—— School.

SOCIAL QUESTIONS

27. The influence of the five-cent theater is beneficial.

28. A state board with power to forbid public exhibition should exercise stage censorship.

29. Children under sixteen years of age should be prohibited from working in confining industries.

30. Children under fourteen years of age should be prohibited from appearing on the stage.

31. A minimum wage for women employees of department stores should be enacted by the state of X——.

32. Public ownership of saloons would be a desirable method of dealing with the liquor problem.

33. The English system of old-age pensions should be adopted by the United States government.

34. Vivisection should be prohibited by law.

35. The publication of court proceedings in criminal and divorce cases should be subject to a board of censorship.

36. Education under the direction of a state board, should be required in the state prisons of X——.

37. The laws of marriage and divorce should be uniform throughout the United States (constitutionality conceded).

38. Local option is the best method of dealing with the liquor question.

39. The army canteen is desirable.

40. A system of compulsory industrial insurance should be adopted by the state of X——.

41. An eight-hour law for all women workers should be enacted by the state of X——.

42. Immigration should be restricted according to the provisions of the Dillingham-Burnett bill.

43. Free employment bureaus should be established by the city of X——.

44. Free employment bureaus should be established by the state of X——.

POLITICAL QUESTIONS

45. A permanent national tariff commission should be established.

46. The constitution should be so amended as to make more easy the passing of amendments.

47. The restrictions on Mongolian immigration should be removed.

48. The President of the United States should serve one term of six years.

49. Complete public reports of all contributions to political campaign funds should be required by law.

50. The Monroe Doctrine as a part of American foreign policy should be discontinued.

51. The interests of labor can best be represented by a separate political party.

52. The naturalization laws of the United States should be made more stringent.

53. Aliens should be forbidden the ballot in every state.

54. The state of California is justified in her stand against land ownership by aliens.

55. Permanent retention of the Philippine Islands by the United States is not advisable.

56. The United States navy should be maintained at a fighting strength equal to any in the world.

57. Direct presidential primaries should be a substitute for the present method of presidential nomination.

58. Corporations engaged in interstate business should be compelled to operate under a national charter.

59. The Panama Canal should be fortified.

60. The initiative and referendum in matters of state legislation would be desirable in the state of X——.

61. From the standpoint of the United States the annexation of Cuba would be desirable.

62. The fifteenth amendment to the Constitution of the United States should be repealed.

63. The President should be elected by the direct vote of the people of the United States.

64. Proportional representation should be adopted in the state of X——.

65. The plan of proportional representation in present vogue in the state of X—— should be abolished.

66. The use of voting machines should be required in all elections in cities having a population of more than 10,000.

67. Public interest is best served when national party lines are discarded in municipal elections.

68. Suffrage should be limited to persons who can read and write.

69. Ex-Presidents of the United States should become senators-at-large for life.

70. Ex-Presidents of the United States should be pensioned for life at full salary.

71. The United States should adopt a plan of compulsory voting.

72. The national government should purchase and operate the express systems in connection with the parcel post.

73. Federal judges should be elected by direct vote of the people.

74. Two-thirds of a jury should be competent to render a verdict in jury trials in the state of X——.

75. The state of X—— should adopt a plan for recall of state judges.

76. The state of X—— should adopt a plan allowing a referendum of judicial decisions.

77. The appointment of United States consuls should be under the merit system.

78. American vessels engaged in coastwise trade should be permitted the use of the Panama Canal without the payment of tolls.

79. All postmasters should be elected by popular vote.

80. The bill requiring ——, which is at present before the X—— city council (X—— state legislature, or Congress) should be defeated.

ECONOMIC AND INDUSTRIAL QUESTIONS

81. The Underwood tariff bill of 1913 would be a desirable law.

82. The federal government should undertake at once the construction of an inland waterway from the Great Lakes to the Gulf (or from X to Y).

83. All raw materials should be admitted to the United States free of duty.

84. A state law should prohibit prison contract labor in the state of X——.

85. Federal government control of all natural resources would be desirable.

86. Municipal ownership of street railways would be an advantage to cities.

87. The Henry George system of single tax would be practicable in the United States.

88. A graduated income tax would be a desirable addition to the federal taxing system.

89. The boycott is a justifiable weapon in labor strikes.

90. The federal government should enact a progressive inheritance tax.

91. The coal mines of the United States should be under federal control.

92. Employers of labor are justified in demanding the "open shop."

93. Irrigation projects to reclaim the arid lands of the West should be undertaken by the United States government.

94. Courts for the compulsory settlement of controversies between labor and capital should be created by Congress.

95. Industrial combinations commonly known as "trusts" are an economical benefit to the United States.

96. The United States should establish and maintain a system of subsidies for the American merchant marine.

97. No tax should be levied on the issue of state banks.

98. Permanent copyrights should be extended by the national government.

99. The judicial injunction as an instrument in labor controversies should be made illegal.

100. A law gradually lowering the present tariff, so that in ten years the United States will be committed to a policy of free trade, would be economically desirable for the United States.

APPENDIX VII

FORMS FOR JUDGES' DECISION

The first of the two following forms is a simple and commonly used one; the second is more formal and is desirable when the schools wish to point out carefully the principles upon which the decision is to be based. A form such as the first, which allows the judge entire freedom, is becoming the more popular.

I.

In my opinion, the better debating has been done by the ——— team.

II

JUDGES' DECISION

[In rendering a decision, the judges are asked to act without reference to their own opinion on the merits of the question. They are not to consider that either contesting party necessarily represents the actual attitude of themselves or of their school. They are to act without consultation. A decision is desired based solely on the quality of debating.

In determining the quality of debating, the judges are asked to consider both matter and form. Grasp of the question, accuracy of analysis, selection of evidence, and order and cogency of arguments should be considered in judging matter. Bearing, voice, directness, earnestness, emphasis, enunciation, and gesture should be considered in judging form.]

DECISION

Considering the above instructions, I cast my ballot for the ——— .